PHILIP ALLAN

LITERATURE GUIDE

FOR A-LEVEL

THE FRENCH LIEUTENANT'S WOMAN

JOHN FOWLES

Series editor: Nicola Onyett

PHILIP ALLAN
UPDATES

Philip Allan Updates, an imprint of Hodder Education, an Hachette UK company, Market Place, Deddington, Oxfordshire OX15 0SE

Orders

Bookpoint Ltd, 130 Milton Park, Abingdon, Oxfordshire OX14 4SB

tel: 01235 827827

fax: 01235 400401

e-mail: education@bookpoint.co.uk

Lines are open 9.00 a.m.–5.00 p.m., Monday to Saturday, with a 24-hour message answering service. You can also order through the Philip Allan Updates website: www.philipallan.co.uk

© Martin Old 2010

ISBN 978-1-4441-1985-5

First printed 2010

Impression number 5 4 3 2 1

Year 2014 2013 2012 2011 2010

Printed in Spain

Hachette UK's policy is to use papers that are natural, renewable and recyclable products and made from wood grown in sustainable forests. The logging and manufacturing processes are expected to conform to the environmental regulations of the country of origin.

P01802

Cover photo: Meryl Streep as Sarah Woodruff in the 1981 film version by Karel Reisz. © KPA/HIP/TopFoto

Contents

Using this guide

Why read this guide?

The purposes of this A-level Literature Guide are to enable you to organise your thoughts and responses to the text, deepen your understanding of key features and aspects and help you to address the particular requirements of examination questions and coursework tasks in order to obtain the best possible grade. It will also prove useful to those of you writing a coursework piece on the text as it provides a number of summaries, lists, analyses and references to help with the content and construction of the assignment.

Note that teachers and examiners are seeking above all else evidence of an *informed personal response to the text*. A guide such as this can help you to understand the text, form your own opinions, and suggest areas to think about, but it cannot replace your own ideas and responses as an informed and autonomous reader.

Chapter and page references in this guide refer to the 2004 Vintage edition of *The French Lieutenant's Woman*.

How to make the most of this guide

You may find it useful to read sections of this guide when you need them, rather than reading it from start to finish. For example, you may find it helpful to read the *Contexts* section before you start reading the text, or to read the *Chapter summaries and commentaries* section in conjunction with the text — whether to back up your first reading of it at school or college or to help you revise. The sections relating to the Assessment Objectives will be especially useful in the weeks leading up to the exam.

Key elements

Look at the Context boxes to find interesting facts that are relevant to the text.

| Context |

Be exam-ready

Broaden your thinking about the text by answering the questions in the **Pause for thought** boxes. These help you to consider your own opinions in order to develop your skills of criticism and analysis.

Pause for **Thought** ❚❚

Build critical skills

Taking it further boxes suggest poems, films, etc. that provide further background or illuminating parallels to the text.

Taking it **Further** ➤

Where to find out more

Use the **Task** boxes to develop your understanding of the text and test your knowledge of it. Answers for some of the tasks are given online, and do not forget to look online for further self-tests on the text.

Task

Test yourself

Follow up cross references to the **Top ten quotations** (see pages 91–93), where each quotation is accompanied by a commentary that shows why it is important.

❮ Top ten *quotation*

Know your text

Don't forget to go online: **www.philipallan.co.uk/literatureguidesonline** where you can find additional exam responses, a glossary of literary terms, interactive questions, podcasts and much more.

Synopsis

It is March 1867: Charles Smithson and his fiancée, Ernestina Freeman ('Tina'), are walking along the Cobb at Lyme Regis when they notice a solitary, mysterious woman staring out to sea. This is Sarah Woodruff — 'The French Lieutenant's Woman'. She is a social outcast considered by many to be slightly mad following a disastrous love affair with and subsequent abandonment by Varguennes, a French officer who was shipwrecked and whom Sarah nursed back to health. Now living with Mrs Poulteney at Marlborough House, Sarah haunts the vicinity of the sea walls, maintaining her isolation from society. The next day Charles goes fossil-hunting in Lyme Undercliff and encounters Sarah sleeping; she wakes up and Charles apologises for disturbing her, notices her fine, dark eyes, and leaves her. After stopping at a dairy, Charles sees Sarah on the path. She rejects his offer to escort her home and asks him to tell no one that she has been walking on Ware Commons, an activity forbidden by Mrs Poulteney. The next day, during a visit to Marlborough House, Sarah notices that both Charles and Ernestina's Aunt Tranter support the burgeoning love affair between Sam, Charles's manservant, and Mary, Mrs Tranter's maid. Charles assumes that he has made a secret connection with Sarah, but the next time their paths cross on the Undercliff, she resists his suggestion that she find a life away from Mrs Poulteney's control, insisting that she cannot leave the area. Charles assumes that she hopes Varguennes may return, but when she admits that the married lieutenant will never do so, Charles, growing tired of Ernestina's shallowness, falls for Sarah's mysterious beauty.

During another walk, Sarah finds Charles, gives him two *Micraster* fossils, and begs him to hear her story. Despite some reservations Charles agrees and Sarah tells him that Varguennes seduced her but that she willingly gave herself to him, revealing that she is now free of the stifling conventions of society and finds some comfort in her shame. During this conversation, Sam and Mary appear, and Sarah and Charles hide. As she watches Sam and Mary embrace, Sarah turns to Charles and smiles. Charles, aware of his sexual attraction to Sarah, says they must never meet alone again, and leaves.

That evening Charles learns he may lose his inheritance as his Uncle Robert is about to marry the widow Bella Tomkins. The news causes Ernestina to behave like 'a draper's daughter', which gives Charles even more reason to doubt the wisdom of his engagement. He learns that

Sarah has been dismissed by Mrs Poulteney for disobeying her walking edict and seeks Dr Grogan's advice about Sarah. Grogan, who believes Sarah to be deranged and in need of asylum care, suggests that Sarah engineered this dismissal so that Charles would come to her rescue, and advises Charles to have nothing more to do with her. Charles, however, chooses not to follow Grogan's advice and meets Sarah the next day in Carslake Barn, where they passionately kiss. Guiltily, Charles breaks away and rushes out of the barn but bumps into Sam and Mary, who have seen them together. The servants promise to keep secret their knowledge of Charles meeting Sarah.

Sarah escapes the threat of the asylum by moving to Exeter. Charles, now in London temporarily, feels increasingly trapped by Ernestina's father, who wants him to become part of his business empire. After a 'debauch', when he engages the services of a prostitute also named Sarah but does not have sex with her, Charles is tempted to go to Sarah but instead returns to Ernestina. Fowles here provides the first of three endings: Charles and Ernestina marry, as do Sam and Mary — a contrived Victorian conclusion. Immediately, however, the narrator reveals that this ending is only what has taken place in Charles's imagination.

Charles does go to Sarah, who seduces him, but Charles is astonished to discover that Sarah was still a virgin and is disorientated by her lies. Following a terse conversation, she orders him to leave her hotel room. After visiting a church where he finally rejects Christianity and duty he returns not to Sarah but to his hotel, where he writes Sarah a letter outlining his plan to marry her. He tells Sam to deliver the letter and the accompanying packet containing a gold brooch. If Sam brings back no reply, Charles will know that Sarah has accepted his proposal of marriage. After breaking off his engagement with Ernestina the next day, Charles returns to Exeter but finds that Sarah has disappeared to London. Sam has evidently stolen the brooch and has not delivered the letter. Later Sam marries Mary.

Charles strenuously tries to find Sarah, and after being forced by Freeman to sign an admission of guilt about his behaviour, he goes to Europe and then America. In February 1869 Mary spots Sarah in London and tells Sam, who now feels guilty about his conduct and anonymously notifies Charles's solicitor about Sarah's whereabouts. Charles gets back to London in May and visits Dante Gabriel Rossetti's house in Chelsea, where Sarah is living. Sarah, surprised to see Charles, tells him she has been working as Rossetti's amanuensis. Charles is shocked at how easily Sarah has embraced the world of the bohemian Pre-Raphaelites. Charles confesses his love but Sarah insists that she will never marry. Charles

prepares to leave. However, Sarah restrains him and says there is a lady in the house who can reveal her true nature. A baby is placed on the carpet and Charles realises that this is his daughter, Lalage, the result of his sexual encounter with Sarah. In this second version of the ending, the three embrace, suggesting that they will become a true family.

The narrator then reappears, sets his watch back fifteen minutes, and provides the third ending to the story. Sarah reasserts her decision not to marry, but suggests that she and Charles might remain friends and perhaps, in time, lovers. Charles, who does not want to become an object of derision to the Pre-Raphaelites and who detects a selfish cruelty in Sarah, who has lied to him yet again, discovers an atom of faith in himself, rejects her offer and leaves.

Chapter summaries and commentaries

Chapter 1

The novel begins in March 1867, as Charles Smithson and Ernestina Freeman walk on the Cobb in Lyme. The elegant couple are well-dressed; she wears 'the height of fashion' (p. 4), a brilliant 'magenta skirt of an almost daring narrowness' (p. 5) in contrast to the figure of a motionless black-clad woman 'apparently leaning against an old cannon-barrel' (p. 5) staring out to sea. This woman (the eponymous French Lieutenant's Woman) appears to be more 'a figure from myth' than a part of petty provincial life.

Commentary: **Fowles mentions the sculptures of Henry Moore (anachronistic to the characters, though, significantly, not to Fowles or his readers) and is unashamedly writing for an educated readership, making unglossed references to the geographical proximity of Athens to its harbour Piraeus, the Spanish Armada, the Monmouth rebellion, Michelangelo,**

TopFoto

An old photo of the Cobb at Lyme Regis

epigraph

a short quotation at the
beginning of a book or
chapter, suggesting its
theme; in *The French
Lieutenant's Woman*
there is at least one for
each chapter.

Taking it
Further

Listen to a modern
interpretation of the song
by Steeleye Span, 'Sails of
Silver', at **www.youtube.
com** (search for Steeleye
Span Sails of Silver).
You can read the lyrics
at **www.hourwolf.com/
steeleye/sails.html**. What
connections can you find
between the heroine of
the song and Sarah in the
novel?

the Middle Ages and 'dundrearies' (elaborate side-whiskers
fashionable until about 1865). The expectation is that the reader
is well enough informed to be able to keep up with its well-
informed writer. Such expectation of reader education would
have been the case for a genuine Victorian novelist. What a
Victorian reader would not have been able to consider would
have been Fowles's use of Freudian symbolism in the positioning
and importance of the upturned phallic cannon to which Sarah
seems so inclined in this opening chapter. Sex, it is clear, will
play a prominent role in this novel.

Chapter 2

The importance of sex is outlined in the **epigraph**, from E. Royston
Pike's *Human Documents of the Victorian Golden Age*, which shows
there were 555,000 more women than men in England around 1851: so
half a million Victorian women were not able to find a marriage partner
or, presumably, sexual fulfilment. The second epigraph, from the folk
song 'As Sylvie was walking' (also known as 'Sails of silver'), cleverly
introduces the idea of a false or faithless lover into the narrative.

Charles and Ernestina banter: the tone is light but the lovers are self-
consciously clever, perhaps as a hallmark of their 'London taste'.
Ernestina informs Charles that the woman is 'poor Tragedy' (p. 9) or 'the
French Lieutenant's Woman', who fell in love with a French sailor who
later abandoned her, leaving her 'a little mad'. Charles, 'without quite
knowing why' (p. 10) talks to the woman about her safety. The woman
turns abruptly to look directly into Charles's eyes, but says nothing.
Charles is struck by the sorrow of the face which is 'not a beautiful face'
but 'unforgettable'. This face contains 'no sign of madness' but will haunt
him for the rest of the novel.

Commentary: **The banter between Charles and Ernestina conveys
important overtones about the novel's plot and themes: Charles
has disagreed with Ernestina's father about Darwin's theory
of evolution; and has been shown symbolically to kneel at the
sight of the fossil *Certhidium portlandicum*. Charles's scientific
credentials are thus established and the key theme of evolution
has been introduced. Ernestina's revulsion at Sarah's reputation
as a fallen woman is not untypical of Victorian attitudes to sex;
however, it is not necessarily insincere. Tragedy is apparent in
Sarah's demeanour. More Freudian imagery is utilised when
Sarah's effect on Charles is 'as a lance' (p. 10).**

Chapter 3

Charles in his hotel room stares at his face in the mirror and takes stock of his life and approaching marriage. His main feelings are of 'obscure defeat' and 'dislocated purpose' (p. 12). The chapter ends with Charles's memory of his uncle saying that he had not found 'the right woman' to marry and Charles's own response, 'I too have been looking for the right girl. And I have not found her.' (p. 18)

Commentary: **Charles's 'distinguishing trait' is 'laziness' (p. 17): he was an 'intelligent idler' and is compared to Byron in his sense of 'ennui' (boredom) but without Byron's outlets of 'genius and adultery'. Yet Charles is likeable, decent, humorous and liberal-minded. Fowles cleverly makes Charles guilty of an act which contributes to the extinction of a species locally when he inadvertently shoots 'one of the last Great Bustards...on Salisbury Plain' (p. 15): he is symbolically shown to be unable to save a species from extinction in Britain. The careful reader will be alerted to the possibility that despite his engagement to Ernestina, she might not be 'right' for Charles.**

Chapter 4

The 'incipient sadists' (p. 20), Mrs Poulteney and Mrs Fairley her 'grim' housekeeper, are introduced. Mrs Poulteney who 'believed in Hell' now fears for her soul and, on the advice of the local vicar, she agrees to take in a woman of 'irreproachable moral character' (p. 25) to act as her companion. Vicar Forsythe suggests Sarah Woodruff.

Commentary: **Fowles satirises Mrs Poulteney's hypocritical malevolence: her kitchen with its fires and remorseless furnaces is a metaphoric hell.**

Chapter 5

In her bedroom Ernestina catches sight of herself in the mirror and narcissistically imagines herself to be someone 'truly...wicked' (p. 29). What follows is 'a sexual thought...that frightened her' due to 'the aura of pain and brutality that the act seemed to require' (pp. 29–30). She banishes the thought by commanding herself 'I must not' and, after opening her diary and crossing out the date so she can count down the days to her marriage, she finds a sprig of jasmine and smells it.

Context

Lord Byron (1788–1824) was a British Romantic poet. Byron's fame has as much to do with his life as his writing: Lady Caroline Lamb claimed he was 'mad, bad and dangerous to know'. He created scandal by his reckless spending, love affairs with men and women, and restless travel. He died of a fever while aiding the Greeks in their war against the Turks. Charles is as well-travelled as Byron, though lacks his poetic gifts (see Chapter 58).

Commentary: **Ernestina is linked symbolically to 'February violets' (p. 26) also found in the words of Ophelia in Shakespeare's *Hamlet* ('I would give you some violets, but they withered all when my father died', IV.5.184–85): and in John Everett Millais's 1852 painting *Ophelia*. The garland of violets around Ophelia's neck symbolises faithfulness but violets can also symbolise chastity and death in the young.**

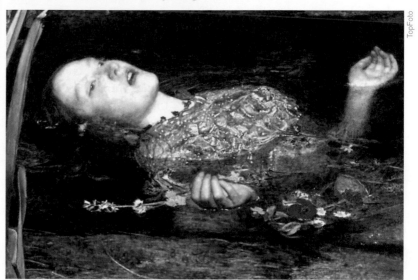

TopFoto

Detail of John Everett Millais's painting *Ophelia*, showing the garland of violets around the drowned girl's neck

Ernestina is a sexual creature but she is repressing her id (see the section on Freud in *Contexts*, pp. 68–71). Jasmine is symbolically significant: attachment, elegance and modesty are its most-often cited qualities but in Japan jasmine is symbolic of the sort of amiability that attracts wealth. These are perfect metaphors for Charles's relationship with Ernestina at this stage of the novel.

Chapter 6

Sarah's arrival at Mrs Poulteney's is described and her history revealed: a farmer's daughter with 'a better education than one would expect' (p. 33) became a governess, found employment with the Talbots and nursed an injured French lieutenant who engaged her affections but abandoned her. The vicar confirms that Sarah is 'not insane…suffers from grave attacks of melancholia…she is slightly crazed' (pp. 35–36). Sarah agrees to becoming Mrs Poulteney's assistant because 'Marlborough House commanded a magnificent prospect of Lyme Bay' and 'She had exactly sevenpence in the world' (p. 38).

Commentary: **Fowles gives us the version of Sarah's history that people in Lyme believe. By placing Sarah with the 'plump vulture' Mrs Poulteney, Fowles foreshadows the trouble that will inevitably develop: Sarah will behave compliantly but will not be drawn on her past. Sarah's poverty is established: Fowles will return to the themes of social class and economics many times.**

Chapter 7

Charles awakes to 'ravishing fragments of Mediterranean warmth' (p. 39), rare for a Lyme March morning. As Charles dresses, he teases his servant, Sam, about never returning to London because of the charms of country life. Charles learns that Sam is growing increasingly fond of the 'nubile' Mary, Aunt Tranter's servant, despite his protestations about her only being a 'milkmaid'. As Charles shaves he is aware of his own 'ambiguous' face.

Commentary: **Marx's epigraph symbolically links Sarah, currently a 'slave' of Mrs Poulteney, to Sam and Mary: though their forms of enslavement differ the reader is invited to question whether the human spirit can flourish under such restraint. The hint is clear: some form of revolution is inevitable. This idea will link to the parallel theme of evolution. Charles's happiness looks complete at the beginning of Chapter 7, but he needs Sam to open the curtains, lay out his clothes, bring his breakfast and even strop (sharpen) his razor. Charles, clearly functionally useless, is emerging as a sort of fossil.**

Chapter 8

When Charles arrives at Aunt Tranter's he learns that Ernestina is indisposed but will be well enough to receive him that afternoon. Giving Sam the rest of the day off — 'not all Victorian employers were directly responsible for communism' (p. 46) — Charles walks to the 'highly fossiliferous' beach area close to Ware Cleeves to hunt for 'tests' (*Echinodermia*) — favourite fossils. His heavy, inappropriate clothing is described. Charles finds a fine example of ammonites embedded in rock, which he designates as a present for Ernestina, and realising that it is too late to return along the shore, he rests before attempting a steep path that leads to the woods above.

Commentary: **Charles's fossil-hunting garb accentuates his attachment to 'duty', but when he paddles we see his 'schoolboy'**

> **Context**
>
> Carl Linnaeus (1707–78) was a Swedish botanist whose major contribution to science was his systematisation of binomial nomenclature — the establishment of universally accepted conventions for the naming of organisms — which became known as Linnaean taxonomy, still widely used in the biological sciences. Darwin completely overturned the Linnaean orthodoxy of '*nulla species nova*' (no new species).

side. Caught in an intellectual contradiction, Charles knows the philosophy of Linnaeus is 'rubbish', yet has not made the intellectual leap that 'if new species *can* come into being, old species very often have to make way for them' (p. 51).

Chapter 9

The melodramatic literature of the period (known as the 'penny dreadful') is mentioned as Mrs Talbot imagines terrible fates for Sarah, including jumping from a cliff to avoid her tormentors. Sarah's background is contextualised in more detail: she was 'doomed to… spinsterhood' (p. 55), yet had found life with Mrs Poulteney at least tolerable. Mrs Poulteney would prefer Sarah not to go walking at all, but if she must, she is not to go to the Cobb. Mrs Fairley reports that Sarah has been walking in the notorious Ware Commons. The careful reader will note that when Charles saw Sarah for the first time she was disobeying the Poulteney edict.

Commentary: **Mrs Talbot's imagined end for Sarah is exaggerated, but not that far short of what could happen to an unlucky Victorian woman involved in a sexual scandal. Sarah, we learn, is 'intelligent' and 'was born with a computer in her heart' (p. 53). Her education is contextualised in Marxist terms: 'Her father had forced her out of her own class, but could not raise her to the next' (p. 54). Her prospects of marriage have been worsened by this arrangement. Sarah is in this context classless, a status which makes her initially vulnerable as an outcast but free from having to conform to Victorian stereotypes. Fowles's claim that Sarah was 'doomed to…spinsterhood' is a clue to her eventual marital destiny.**

Top ten *quotation* 〉

Sarah is… classless… vulnerable as an outcast but free from having to conform to Victorian stereotypes

Chapter 10

The verdant micro-climate of the Undercliff is described as a place of 'anti-science' (p. 68). Charles's earlier happiness has been replaced by a 'malaise'. Gradually his scientific nature reasserts itself and when exploring he discovers a woman lying below him on a little shelf of rock. Moving closer, he recognises the sleeping Sarah who wakes with a start. Charles apologises and leaves Sarah alone.

Commentary: **The Undercliff, an 'English Garden of Eden' (p. 67), serves as a mysterious wilderness where magical things can and do happen, linking it to the 'domaine' described by Alain-**

Fournier in *Le Grand Meaulnes*. Sarah's position while sleeping is tender yet sexual. The importance of this chance encounter is described in epoch-changing terms: although Charles did not know it, 'the whole Victorian age was lost' (p. 72).

Chapter 11

At the same time as Charles and Sarah meet, Ernestina moodily re-reads that morning's diary entry. After admonishing Mary about her conduct with Sam she opens her diary at the page with the jasmine sprig. There follows a section on how Charles and Ernestina met. Ernestina was 'wildly determined…to have Charles' (p. 80), who had spent the two years since his last travels 'in a state of extreme sexual frustration' (p. 82) and woke up one morning believing that he loved Ernestina. She accepted his proposal but when they kissed it was 'chastely' and accompanied not by mistletoe but by the ubiquitous jasmine.

Commentary: **Charles's sexual frustration is important: his asexual kiss with Ernestina will not give him the passion he craves.**

The passing mention of Mary's world-famous great-great-granddaughter (p. 75) shows the reader that the world is not locked forever in a system which forbids social and geographical mobility; in Marxist and Darwinian terms the world is evolving.

Chapter 12

Charles stops at a dairy and, seeing Sarah, asks the farmer if he knows who she is. The dairyman replies, 'She be the French Loot'n'nt's Hoer' (p. 86). This angers Charles, who runs after Sarah. Charles offers to escort Sarah home but she refuses, asking him not to tell anyone that he has seen her. Charles stops at Aunt Tranter's but remains silent about his encounter with Sarah. Meanwhile Mrs Poulteney has discovered that Sarah has been walking in Ware Commons and warns her not to go there again. Later Sarah is shown to be standing crying at her bedroom window, perhaps contemplating suicide.

Commentary: **Charles's obsession with Sarah is growing: he feels chivalrous, wanting to demonstrate that 'not everybody in her world was a barbarian' (p. 86) — see *Contexts* on Heraclitus (p. 66 of this guide). Sarah's face profoundly affects Charles: 'after each sight of it, he could not believe its effect, and had to see it again' (p. 86). The fossil that Charles gives to Ernestina is**

too heavy for her to hold — a symbolic reference to Charles's and Ernestina's irreconcilable differences, perhaps. The chapter ends with 'Who is Sarah? Out of what shadows does she come?' (p. 94)

Chapter 13

Fowles claims he does not know who Sarah is or out of which shadows she comes. The story and the characters are all imaginary and he has 'pretended' up to now that they behave at his behest, but he has read Roland Barthes and claims that the characters take on lives and personalities of their own. Sarah did not kill herself and continued to haunt Ware Commons but Fowles says he does not know why.

Commentary: **This chapter is an essay on the craft of the Postmodern novelist: everything is fiction, even our 'real' lives, which we self-censor and dress up in a 'romanced autobiography' (p. 96). For a definition and explanation of Postmodernism, see the *Form, structure and language* section of this guide, pp. 57–59.**

Chapter 14

Charles again encounters Sarah, this time at Mrs Poulteney's home. Mrs Poulteney attempts to discuss Mary's allegedly inappropriate behaviour with Sam, but Aunt Tranter defends her. Ernestina sides with Mrs Poulteney and Charles defends Mrs Tranter: Charles and Sarah exchange a meaningful, secret glance about their 'common enemy', Mrs Poulteney, and Charles decides he will need to talk to Sam and 'teach Ernestina an evidently needed lesson in common humanity' (p. 106). During this awkward social call, Sam and Mary are having a serious, though undisclosed, conversation in the kitchen.

Commentary: **Charles's common decency is again outlined as he defends Mary's and Sam's conduct and we see a vindictive side to Ernestina's nature which Charles finds displeasing. The look between Charles and Sarah 'spoke worlds...For the first time she did not look through him, but at him' (p. 106). The sub-plot concerning Sam and Mary becomes more dominant.**

Chapter 15

Ernestina apologises to Charles for siding with Mrs Poulteney. Forgiven, she gets a fit of the giggles and tries to atone by giving her 'green walking-dress' to Mary. Later Charles teases Sam about sending him back to London but advises him to be careful and not to break Mary's heart.

Commentary: **When Charles accepts Ernestina's apology he says that she is a 'sweet child' and that she 'will always be that' to him (p. 108). The 'always' is vital: the relationship between Charles and Ernestina will be of permanent inequality. Charles's and Ernestina's shared insight about the freedoms of the age is ironic. They have not realised that freedom leads to choices which might be harmful. Sam defends his behaviour with Mary by claiming 'We're not 'orses. We're 'ooman beings' (p. 110). Despite his kindness and sense of justice, Charles will suffer later due to his insistence on treating Sam more like a lackey than a human being.**

Chapter 16

Freed from domestic tedium, Charles returns to his 'wretched grubbing' (p. 117) and heads for the spot in the woods where he last saw Sarah, whom he discovers. When they hear poachers Sarah hides. Charles comforts Sarah, advising her to leave Lyme, and offers financial assistance, but Sarah claims 'I cannot leave this place' (p. 123). When Varguennes is mentioned Sarah says, 'I know he will never return…He is married!' (pp. 124–25). She disappears, leaving Charles alone.

Commentary: **There is much reference to Freud in this chapter: the writer expects his readers to be familiar with the term 'super-ego' to complement the 'id' of Chapter 5. Charles's awareness of Sarah is more sexual: 'he now guessed darker qualities' (p. 120). Madame Bovary is mentioned and the name is a 'temptation' as well as a 'comprehension' to Charles, who chooses to remain and force Sarah to talk. Charles, the palaeontologist, wants to discover as many sedimentary layers of Sarah's character as possible, but when she does talk he is left in 'amazement' and understands her no better than when he began to chip away. Her eyes (once again) both repel and lance him and he begins to feel guilt; Fowles leaves him unable to solve the enigma that is Sarah.**

Chapter 17

During a concert, Charles is 'free to examine his conscience' (p. 128) and his thoughts wander to the contrast between Sarah, with whom he acknowledges 'he had become a little obsessed' (p. 128) and 'vapid'

Context

Gustave Flaubert's novel *Madame Bovary* (1856) tells of an unhappily married middle-class doctor's wife who seeks escape through adultery and living beyond her means. The novel is an exposé of the situation of women like Emma Bovary, whose lives were stiflingly dull but who were tied to their husbands and a life of duty. Now a classic feminist and social realist text, *Madame Bovary* was the subject of a court case under France's obscenity laws and became a best-seller when the prosecution case collapsed.

Taking it **Further**

For a coursework assignment exploring the dark undercurrents of love, compare *The French Lieutenant's Woman* with *Madame Bovary* and one of Shakespeare's plays — *Antony and Cleopatra* or *Measure for Measure* or *Troilus and Cressida*.

Ernestina, who now represents his own future not as of 'vast potential' but as 'a fixed voyage to a known place' (p. 130). Sam's and Mary's relationship is further described.

Commentary: **The author reminds us of his presence via the comparison of the Assembly Rooms then and now. Sam's dreams are revealed: he wants to be a haberdasher and Mary is now an active part of this dream, not a passive passenger in the manner of Ernestina in Charles's languid life. The reader may infer that Ernestina may dilute some of Charles's better qualities but that Mary will add to Sam's happiness.**

Chapter 18

Charles goes to Ware Commons again and after finding a rather poor example of *Echinocorys scutata* he becomes intuitively aware of Sarah staring at him. 'Truly beautiful', her face possesses 'an inner as well as outer light' (p. 139). Sarah gives Charles excellent *Micraster* tests and thanks Charles for his previous offer of help, confessing that she has 'no one to turn to' (p. 140) and that she cannot go to London because she will be forced into prostitution. Sarah begs him to meet her again and he reluctantly agrees. Charles leaves feeling lost and lured.

Commentary: **It is clear that Sarah has been following Charles, and though it is not a windy day 'her hair was loose' (p. 138) as if deliberately so. There is a religious quality about Sarah's appearance, but to illustrate her dual nature, Fowles utilises sinister symbolism via the ivy and 'entombing greenery' (p. 139) that surrounds her. Sarah's assumption of equality of intellect shocks Charles and her 'incomprehension' that society has been so unjust as to make Miss Freeman able to do things denied to Sarah bewilders Charles. The owl hooting during the daytime is symbolic of some imminent act of doom and Charles knows he is 'about to engage in the forbidden, or rather the forbidden was about to engage in him' (p. 147). Metaphorically Charles is teetering on the brink of an abyss.**

Chapter 19

After dinner at the White Lion, Charles goes to Dr Grogan's. Among political and scientific topics they discuss Sarah, whom Grogan diagnoses as suffering from melancholia, based on the theories of 'a clever German doctor' (p. 155). At the same time, the author reveals that

Sarah is currently asleep in bed, her arm thrown over the body of the servant Millie. The two women behave as innocently 'as sisters'. Grogan and Charles talk about Lyell, Darwin and Gosse (explained in the hilarious footnote on *Omphalos*) before they confide in each other that they are passionate 'Darwinians'. Charles, full of self-confidence, leaves for his hotel.

Commentary: **Fowles gives us Grogan's scientific view of Sarah directly after the chapter where Sarah has given her own view of herself. This enables the reader (and Charles) to consider whether Sarah is 'deranged' or a victim of a cruel society, as she herself seems to believe. The vignette about Sarah and the 'sickly lamb' Millie is used to explore different sociological and historical attitudes to lesbianism. Incomprehension has been mentioned three times now in two chapters: Sarah cannot comprehend her treatment in society; Charles cannot comprehend that a person can be addicted to melancholy and Mrs Poulteney cannot comprehend lesbianism. The effect on the reader is to show that there are some things in this novel that are *not to be understood* and that will remain mysteries. An important clue for later in the novel (Chapter 60) is given by Fowles on the subject of lesbianism: Sarah is 'ignorant' of it and it is not to her natural tastes. Ironically, when Charles leaves Grogan's he believes that he has been 'naturally selected', that he has 'pure intellect…free as a god…understanding all' (p. 163). The final phrase of the chapter ('All except Sarah, that is', p. 163) shows how wrong-headed Charles is about his faith in himself as one of 'the lords of creation' (p. 160). Fowles's mockery of Charles and his unthinking sexism has become a little more caustic by this stage of the novel.**

Context

Melancholia: 'Dr Hartmann' is Fowles's amusing idea of a pre-Freudian Freud. By the 1860s the terms 'depression' and 'melancholia' were being used to refer to a physiological and metaphorical lowering of emotional function. Since Aristotle, melancholia had been associated with men of intellectual brilliance; However, the newer concept 'depression' abandoned this association and became more associated with women. Subsequently the term 'melancholia' dropped out of use.

Chapter 20

Charles again finds Sarah at the end of the tunnel of ivy and hears her story: she had fallen in love with Varguennes at the Talbots' and visited him in Weymouth once he had recovered. She claims she knew Varguennes was insincere and though her mind was confused she wished to appear to be the mistress of her destiny, and so 'gave' herself to him. In doing so, she 'married shame' so that people should point at her and stare, saying: 'There walks the French Lieutenant's Whore' (p. 175). Charles imagines himself as Varguennes, glimpsing the dark shadows.

Commentary: **Sarah is again unbonneted and deliberately allows Charles to see the 'bottoms of her pantalettes' (p. 166) as she walks up the bank: Sarah is once again in charge of the situation, leading. Symbolic primroses, violets and wild strawberries carpet the floor of the dell. There is a major shift in the sexual key of their relationship following Sarah's confession: Charles simultaneously forgives her and wants her; he hates Varguennes and wants to be him. The Pre-Raphaelite Brotherhood is mentioned via the paintings of John Everett Millais and Ford Madox Brown, who wanted to admit 'nature and sexuality' into their work. Charles, surrounded by nature, is struggling to repress his sexual feelings for Sarah.**

Context

The Pre-Raphaelite Brotherhood was a group of English painters, poets and critics, founded in 1848 by William Holman Hunt, John Everett Millais and Dante Gabriel Rossetti. The group believed that classical artists like Raphael had corrupted art and they aimed to capture the spirit of earlier painters — hence the name — and were thus attracted to vibrant colours and medieval themes. In the final chapters of the novel Rossetti's and Sarah's lives become entwined.

Top ten *quotation* ❯

Task *1*

Research the symbolism of the other plants and flowers in this section to learn more about the natural symbolism of the novel.

Chapter 21

Sarah continues her confession: Varguennes left the day after having sex with Sarah; she learned a month later he was married and wrote back to him saying she never wished to see him again. She reiterates that she wants to be an 'outcast', claiming England is full of 'Outcasts who are afraid to seem so' (p. 180). Charles repeats his advice that she must leave Lyme, and she deliberately cuts her finger on a hawthorn branch. Charles believes that her 'Confession had brought cure' (p. 183), as Grogan intimated it might. Charles and Sarah are interrupted by the noise of Sam and Mary laughing nearby. Charles and Sarah hide and Sarah smiles a smile 'so complex' it leaves Charles staring at her 'incredulously' (p. 186). Charles is almost overwhelmed by his sexual desire for Sarah.

Commentary: **In Celtic mythology, the hawthorn is a sacred tree connected to the Fairy Queen, transformed under early Christianity into the Queen of the May. To pagans it symbolises sexual fertility and abandonment but its thorns reveal hidden dangers. Sarah leaves 'lightly', as though pleased with herself for what has been achieved: Charles has admitted his sexual attraction to her ('We must never meet alone again', p. 187) and though she has tacitly agreed to leave Lyme on Charles's advice, she has been granted a day or two to 'reflect'. As Charles watches her go he notices her face has 'its old lancing look again' (p. 188).**

Chapter 22

Charles knows he has been 'playing with fire' (p. 189), but as he has 'escaped unscathed' he feels exhilarated as he sees the Cobb. Consigning

Sarah to 'his past', he feels self-congratulatory. When he arrives at his hotel he finds a telegram from his uncle summoning him to Winsyatt urgently. Charles believes his uncle will hand over either Winsyatt itself or the Elizabethan manor house in the village as a wedding present. He visits Ernestina, who is 'plainly vexed' that Uncle Robert should 'act the grand vizir in this way' (p. 191), but 'a vision of herself, Lady Smithson in a Winsyatt appointed to her taste' (p. 193) appeals to her and Charles is allowed to leave.

Commentary: **'Free will' features seven times in paragraphs two and three: Charles, still believing that he is a 'highly intelligent being, one of the fittest' (p. 190), has faith in his abilities to choose and therefore to consign Sarah to his past. The Darwinian overtones are obvious but Fowles shows that Charles's faith in himself is again false. He reveals Charles's 'greatest defect' in this chapter: though dimly aware of Sarah's 'passion', his mind-set has not equipped him to believe that women could have 'imagination' beyond the merely fanciful: 'those two qualities of Sarah's were banned by the epoch' (p. 190). The plot twist concerning Winsyatt allows Fowles's presentation of Ernestina as a vacuous nonentity to gather momentum as her differences from the 'remarkable' Sarah become clearer.**

Chapter 23

When Charles arrives at Winsyatt he notices that the 'immortal bustard had been banished' (p. 198), but does not guess at the significance of its removal. The reader learns that the previous afternoon on her way back to Lyme, Sarah deliberately made sure that she was observed in the vicinity of the Dairy by Mrs Fairley.

Commentary: **The hand of Mrs Bella Tomkins is visible in the new decor: a radical (r)evolutionary factor is about to enter Winsyatt. The use of the word 'domaine' is a homage to *Le Grand Meaulnes*: Charles's Winsyatt domaine is indeed lost 'but still he did not guess it' (p. 198). The references to Charles entering into his inheritance and 'Duty' being his real wife are ironic: all is about to change. Sarah's deliberate choice to emerge 'in full view' shows that her powers of imagination described in Chapter 22 are being utilised.**

Context

Free will is the supposed ability of people to make choices free from constraints. The question of free will has been a central concern since the beginning of philosophical enquiry. Those who believe in God argue that he is omniscient; so the problem of free will is how our actions can be free if there is a being who has determined them for us ahead of time.

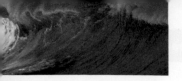

Chapter 24

Charles tells Ernestina about his uncle's engagement to Mrs Tomkins, then asks about the day's events in Lyme. It is disclosed that Mrs Poulteney has dismissed Sarah. Although Sarah has left her things at the White Lion, she has gone missing and a search party is looking for her. The chapter ends with the ominous threat of thunder as Charles walks to his hotel.

Commentary: **The plot twist about the possibility of Charles's disinheritance is important: in Darwinian terms Bella Tomkins is a creature more fitted to survive than Charles, whose aristocratic gallantry in the face of the threat is unrealistic and naive: 'There is no suspicion of fortune-hunting' (p. 201), but Ernestina can recognise another social climber when she sees one. The news that Sarah is 'missing' moves the narrative into a genuinely suspenseful phase where plot becomes as important as themes and ideas.**

Chapter 25

Charles finds a note from Sarah, apparently written the day before, begging him to see her 'one last time', soon followed by a second note written in haste in 'governess French' (p. 209) which can be translated thus: 'I have waited for you all day. I beg you — a woman on her knees implores you to come to her rescue in her despair. I will pass the night praying for your coming. I will be from dawn at the little barn beside the sea reached by the first path on the left after the farm.' Greatly agitated, Charles crumples up the note but wonders about Sarah's welfare, especially now the storm has started. Charles tells Sam, who brings the second note, that he has interested himself in 'an unfortunate woman's case' (p. 208). He hopes to establish her in a 'situation more suited to her abilities' as a 'little surprise' for Mrs Tranter, who must not be told anything about the matter. Sam is instructed to tell no one. Determined that he must talk to someone, Charles leaves the hotel, telling Sam that he may have the supper he was bringing up for him.

Commentary: **Charles has an epiphany (sudden revelation) of understanding, a vivid, black insight: 'all life was parallel... evolution was not vertical, ascending to a perfection, but horizontal. Time was the great fallacy; existence was without history...always this being caught in the same fiendish machine'**

Context

Sarah's language seems to reveal her own view of herself as a wronged woman waiting for a knight in shining armour to 'rescue' her. The references to begging and praying show that Sarah views herself as a lady from a medieval courtly love romance. For a visual image of this idea, see www.jwwaterhouse.com and follow Paintings — *Lamia (on her knees)*.

PHILIP ALLAN LITERATURE GUIDE **FOR A-LEVEL**

(p. 207). Charles is close to acknowledging his Existentialist dilemma: he is no more than a ninety million-year-old ammonite in some recession of water caught in his own micro-catastrophe. (For a definition and explanation of Existentialism, see 'Critical context', pp. 77–79 of this guide.) Charles's desperation to act to show he was 'more than an ammonite' (p. 210) marks the embryonic beginnings of his Existentialist rebellion. Yet Charles could appear to be misguided: he has not arrived to comfort Sarah after the first note when he was at Winsyatt but she has broken her promise never to trouble him again if he did not come. Charles ignores Sam, which will have repercussions.

Chapter 26

Sam contemplates blackmailing Charles about his involvement with Sarah. The chapter concludes with a reprise of what happened the day Charles's uncle told him about his forthcoming marriage: both men felt guilty — the uncle for what he was doing to Charles and the nephew for not having been sufficiently dutiful in the past. On the way back to Lyme, Charles's thoughts turned to Ernestina, to whom he now feels inferior because of her 'massive marriage portion' (p. 219).

Commentary: **The section on Sam, though it identifies him as a 'rat' and Charles as the 'sinking ship', offers some explanation of Sam's motives: he loves Mary; he is poor and because his life-chances are linked to Charles's prospects, he has suffered a reversal of fortune every bit as significant as Charles has. The Victorian class system dehumanised servants, making them 'little more than furniture' (p. 213). Charles's discomfort at now becoming Ernestina's inferior proves that much of his generosity in the early part of the novel about her birth and background was not quite genuine.**

Chapter 27

Charles goes to Grogan for advice; the doctor is 'amazed' to discover that Sarah has sent Charles a note. After calling off the search, he offers his résumé of Charles's entanglement with Sarah, building on his hypothesis in Chapter 19: Sarah's despair is a sort of disease of the mind. Deranged, she has fallen in love with being a victim of fate and she uses her only weapon, the pity she inspires in Charles, to lure

him. She deliberately made sure she was spotted coming out of Ware Commons by Mrs Fairley to ensure her dismissal. Her disappearance is to make people think she is about to throw herself off the nearest cliffs before crying to her 'saviour for help' (p. 224). Grogan knows that Charles is infatuated and if he continues to see Sarah his life and marriage to Ernestina will be compromised, so he offers to meet Sarah in Charles's place and then help Sarah get the treatment she needs at an asylum. He then gives Charles reading material about the trial of Émile de La Roncière.

Commentary: **Grogan's wisdom allows a different view of Sarah to emerge: she is not wicked but wracked with despair. Highly dangerous, she has deliberately set out to use Charles: his choice of the word 'weapon' shows how serious a threat he thinks she is, despite the fact that she has no grand plan: 'She lives from day to day' (p. 225). He identifies Sarah as having 'eyes a man could drown in' (p. 226), thereby demonstrating that other men than Charles have found her remarkable. The digression on de La Roncière is important in the novel, which has now reached its halfway point.**

Chapter 28

Fowles gives us his version of the strange case of Émile de La Roncière and Marie de Morell who lied, forged letters, self-harmed and fabricated crime-scene evidence as a consequence of repressed sexual desire. After Charles has finished reading he becomes extremely agitated and begins pacing the room, 'searching his soul' (p. 238). Once again he equates action with a solution: 'If only he could *act*' (p. 238). Thinking that he has condemned Sarah in order to avoid condemning himself in front of Grogan, Charles decides he must meet Sarah despite the doctor's warning.

Commentary: **This is a pivotal chapter: Fowles explains 'hysteria... caused by sexual repression' (p. 233) via a series of skilfully interwoven strands taken from French and German sources, some of which Fowles translates himself. De La Roncière was the victim of a gross miscarriage of justice and Grogan is warning Charles that Sarah is suffering from the same sort of mental disorder as the women in the case studies. However, reading about them has the opposite effect on Charles, whose Victorianism will not allow him to believe that 'such perversions' as Marie de Morell's existed, especially 'in the pure and sacred sex' (p. 237).**

Chapter 29

Charles walks through the Undercliff, which exudes a 'druid balm' (p. 241) from which he feels excluded. He hears a tiny wren trilling 'its violent song' (p. 242). He reaches the barn and hesitates for a few moments before venturing into the dark, where he sees a black bonnet hanging from a hook. Feeling an 'icy premonition' (p. 244), Charles peers over the partition.

Commentary: **Charles's Existentialist ennui stifles any capacity for the celebration of Nature. Since Charles cannot appreciate the wren's beauty (even on an evolutionary level), his slavish adherence to Christian ideas of sacrifice and duty are shown still to possess him. Is Sarah a shape-shifter (a being with the ability to change its physical form) like the Fairy Queen? Is Charles to be a sacrifice? He is afraid of what he may find in the barn. The novel is once more charged with excitement.**

Chapter 30

The novelist breaks up the narrative flow once again, this time to describe what happened in Sarah's final interview with Mrs Poulteney when she was dismissed for walking in Ware Commons.

Commentary: **The short diversion into Sarah's recent past may well heighten the tension of Chapter 29 for some readers, but others may see it as another unnecessary Postmodern detour. Mrs Poulteney's cold and hypocritical Christianity is contrasted with Sarah's more natural understanding of God.**

Chapter 31

Charles feels a strong sexual urge when he discovers Sarah sleeping: she wakes up and Charles tells her of the search-party, the asylum plan and why she must leave Lyme. Sarah confesses that she has told Charles a lie and that she made sure Mrs Fairley saw her. Charles struggles to understand, despite his recent knowledge about 'distinguished young ladies who had gone in for house-burning and anonymous letter-writing' (p. 252) and worse. As Charles raises Sarah from the ground he can resist no longer and kisses her but before he completely surrenders to sexual passion he 'pushed her violently away' as if he were 'the most debased criminal caught in his most abominable crime' (p. 253). As he rushes through the door someone other than Grogan is standing there.

Context

The Druids considered the wren supreme among birds and used its beautiful music in divination. In Graeco-Roman mythology it symbolises the victory of cleverness over strength, simple joy in life and shared male and female responsibilities in child-rearing. The shape-shifting Fairy Queen often takes the form of a wren. The wren was hunted on St Stephen's Day (26 December) by young men and boys (Wrenboys) who would kill a wren as a reminder of Christ's sacrifice.

Commentary: **The epigraph from Clough is fascinating: is sexual contact spiritual or merely vulgar? Sarah has the same wildness about her as the wren — surely a clue to her shape-shifting abilities. Both characters are feeling 'intense repressed emotion' and as he looks into her 'wide…drowning eyes' they are 'the most ravishingly beautiful he had ever seen' (p. 252). The kiss is inevitable: the destiny of 'those eyes'. Charles's equation of his sexual urges with crime proves that though 'The moment overcame the age' (p. 252), it did so only temporarily and that Charles the ammonite is still marooned in his receding pool. The mysterious identity of the person beyond the barn door is genuinely suspenseful.**

Top ten *quotation* ❯

Chapter 32

Context

In the Victorian Church of England marriage service the woman had to promise obedience to her husband. This vow found its way into the Book of Common Prayer via St Paul's letter to the Ephesians (5:22), which claimed that it was necessary for 'wives to submit to their husbands as to the Lord'.

Ernestina's and Sam's activities are described. Ernestina is guilty about her earlier behaviour concerning Charles possibly losing Winsyatt and writes in her diary that she needs to take the words of the marriage service seriously and obey Charles even when her feelings drive her to contradict him. Sam learns that Charles has left orders that he must pack and be ready to leave the hotel at noon. He visits Mary with the bad news, at which she collapses into tears. However, Mrs Tranter agrees to give Mary three hours off to be with Sam.

Commentary: **Again Charles's and Sarah's narrative is interrupted by what other characters are doing. We learn that Ernestina's diary is for both Charles's eyes and God's, and like other characters (Sarah and Charles in particular) Ernestina has 'several voices' (p. 256). We are promised Ernestina's long-term future with Charles and Charles's 'infidelity', which up to now has only gone as far as a kiss. Fowles is teasing once again.**

Chapter 33

Charles has encountered Sam and Mary, who are at Carslake Barn for a sexual rendezvous. Charles attempts to pay Sam, who has just glimpsed the 'wild' Sarah, but Sam declines the money, assuring Charles that he and Mary will remain silent. When they walk away they 'dissolve into a helpless paralysis of silent laughter' (p. 259). After confessing that all she lives for is to see Charles, Sarah promises to take his advice and go to Exeter. Charles murmurs 'I shall never forget you' (p. 262) before leaving her to her long walk to pick up the coach at Axmouth Cross nine miles away.

Commentary: **Sam and Mary now know something about Charles which may be of use to Sam's blackmail plans. Charles's sense of duty prevails and he apologises to Sarah ('abashed', 'no longer wild') for taking 'unpardonable advantage' of her 'unhappy situation' (p. 261) and gives money, which she accepts with gratitude. Will duty send him back to Ernestina or will he encounter the enigmatic Sarah and her lancing eyes again?**

Chapter 34

Charles tells Ernestina that it is 'imperative' that he leaves for London that day to see Montague his solicitor and Ernestina's father to inform him of what has happened over his inheritance. Ernestina, put out, states she wants to write a letter to her father with strict orders to send Charles straight back to Lyme. Charles promises to give the letter to Mr Freeman and tells Ernestina he will return as soon as possible. As he leaves he finds Mary standing by the door and, ascertaining that she understands from Sam 'the circumstances of this morning' (p. 267), he gives her a gold coin.

Commentary: **Though the meeting is 'stiff', Charles manages to feel a 'distinct stir in his loins' for 'sugar Aphrodite' Ernestina when they kiss on the mouth, fantasising about Ernestina's 'promise of certain buried wildnesses' (p. 267). Yet Charles's dominant feeling is of pollution: the fact that he can 'feel carnal desire now, when he had touched another woman's lips that morning' upsets him. Ernestina is shown to be wilful and obstinate. She 'inwardly seethed'; harbours multiple resentments, is sarcastic and shows a 'very plain and mutinous disagreement' (p. 265). Though she plays along with the idea of being obedient, she knows 'a time would come when Charles should be made to pay for his cruelty' (p. 266). In this vignette Fowles gives us an insight into what Charles's and Ernestina's married life would really be like. Charles's habit of offering money to those he considers his social inferiors impedes his chances of long-term survival and shows his guilty conscience. Fowles gives a Marxist interpretation of the function of charity in a capitalist society: the haves only give to the have-nots to alleviate their guilt at systematically exploiting them. It is clear that Charles is careering into three potential dangers: those outlined by Darwin, Freud and Marx.**

Taking it **Further** ➤

On www.youtube.com watch the video-montage of *The French Lieutenant's Woman* set to the song 'Polly' by Kate Rusby (search for Polly French Lieutenant's Woman). The song lyrics are available at lyrics.wikia.com/Kate_Rusby:Polly. How successfully does the song capture Sarah's nature in the novel?

Charles is careering into three potential dangers: those outlined by Darwin, Freud and Marx

Chapter 35

This chapter is an essay on Victorian values and sexuality (see *Themes*, pp. 50–52 of this guide).

Commentary: **Fowles identifies the essential tensions of the Victorian age: 'lust' versus 'renunciation', 'lyrical surrender' against 'tragic duty', the struggle between 'the sordid facts and their noble use' (p. 275). In this he takes Hardy's life as an emblem and in Tryphena sees Sue Bridehead and Tess of the d'Urbervilles. Beyond the digression we are meant to see the figure of Sarah caught on a rack of repressed sexuality.**

Chapter 36

Exeter and its 'wicked amenities' are described; it is 'notoriously a place to hide' for 'undone girls and women' (p. 276) of the villages and small towns of Devon and Dorset. Endicott's Family Hotel is such a place and we learn that Sarah has been residing there for several days. She unwraps three parcels, containing a nightgown, a dark-green shawl and a roll of bandage. Enjoying 'the first holiday of her adult life' (p. 281): she opens a last parcel, 'a small meat pie', which she begins to eat 'with no delicacy whatsoever' (p. 282).

Commentary: **Charles's ten sovereigns have the power to make Sarah 'contented with her lot' (p. 282). The nightgown, shawl and bandage are very important plot clues but Fowles tells the reader that he has no intention of finding out what is going on in Sarah's mind other than revealing that she is very far from being unhappy.**

Context

A sovereign was a gold coin worth one pound. If we compare the worth of the money then with now, using the Retail Price Index, Charles's ten sovereigns would be worth approximately £646. However, if we use average earnings as a guide, ten sovereigns in 1867 would be worth £5,580 today (data supplied by the Economic History Association).

Chapter 37

Charles has his interview with the 'grave headmasterly' (p. 284) capitalist Mr Freeman, who overcomes his initial thoughts that Charles wants to ask for a bigger dowry. He reads his daughter's letter and accepts the change in Charles's circumstances with some 'kindness' before opening his heart on another matter, offering Charles a partnership in his business. Charles feels he has somehow now become Freeman's 'employee' and is appalled: 'gentlemen cannot go into trade' (p. 290). Telling Freeman that he is 'overwhelmed', he promises to give the matter 'Most serious thought' (p. 291).

Commentary: **Charles's aristocratic background makes him react with horror to Freeman's offer of work. Ironically, despite his disagreements with Charles about evolution ('You will never get me to agree that we are all descended from monkeys'), Freeman understands 'the purpose of this theory of evolution', while Charles the Darwinist does not: 'In order to survive...[a species] must adapt itself to changes in the environment' (p. 290). Charles is presented as an example of an endangered species once again.**

Chapter 38

Charles, 'alien and unhappy' (p. 293) and wishing to be free of his current plight, gets lost in the maze of London streets before by 'fatal coincidence' (p. 296) emerging at Freeman's 'behemoth' of a store in Oxford Street. Believing that 'If I ever set foot in that place I am done for' (p. 297), Charles hails a cab to go somewhere to indulge in 'a bowl of milk punch and a pint of champagne' (p. 299).

Commentary: **Charles is described as 'a poor living fossil' (p. 293), but Fowles asks his readers to see him as 'struggling to overcome history' rather than given to 'futile snobbery' (p. 298).**

Chapter 39

At his club, Charles meets Sir Thomas Burgh, a 'whoring' baronet, and Nathaniel, a bishop's son. Charles gets drunk and accompanies Tom and Nat to Ma Terpsichore's high-class brothel. Unbidden, Sarah's face floats into Charles's mind and, remembering 'the kiss', Charles thinks that he knows what 'all his troubles were caused by...He needed a last debauch' (p. 304). He wanted to do something completely 'unFreemanish'. The sexual entertainment in Ma Terpsichore's repels Charles, who senses that 'there was a despair behind the fixed suggestive smiles of the performers. One was a child who could only have just reached puberty' (p. 308). So he leaves and takes a cab, intending to go home, but stops when he sees a prostitute who looks like Sarah. Despite his belief that it was six hundred to one that she 'did not' (presumably Fowles means 'did') have syphilis he engages her 'all night'. 'His fate was sealed. He wished it so' (p. 311).

Commentary: **That Charles was 'revolted' at the desperation and youth of one of the sex workers shows his strong sense of morality, but his weakness is also shown by his self-loathing and his hiring of the prostitute. Charles and Sarah have been**

Taking it **Further** ▶

On www.youtube.com watch the clip 'An Understanding of Class' from the 1966 TV show *The Frost Report* (search for Frost Report Understanding Class); then watch the 'Upper Class Twit of the Year' sketch from *Monty Python's Flying Circus* (search for Monty Python Upper Class Twit). In what ways do you think that these two comedy sketches fit into Fowles's view of social class in Britain?

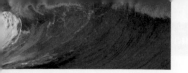

shown inhabiting two very different economic worlds between Chapters 36 and 39: Sarah is content with ten sovereigns but Charles cannot be happy with £2,500 a year and the promise of a business empire. Careful readers will note that Charles pays the prostitute for a night's work one-tenth of what he gave to Sarah.

Chapter 40

Charles pays for the hansom and follows the prostitute into a 'shabby but spotlessly clean' room. Charles hears 'the faint mutter of an awakened child' (p. 313) and the prostitute looks in to shush her 'little gel'. The prostitute sends an errand-boy for wine and food and tells Charles that the baby's father is 'a sojjer…in Hindia now' (p. 314). After her pathetic meal the prostitute changes into a peignoir and sits on Charles's lap. When she kisses him, 'her mouth tasted faintly of onions' (p. 316). Charles's feelings of nausea get stronger. The prostitute gets into bed and after Charles finds that her name is Sarah, he vomits into the pillow.

Commentary: **Charles is sympathetic to the plight of the prostitute, whose essential purity is conveyed via colour symbolism: her peignoir and shawl are both white: she has been wronged and driven to prostitution so she can look after her child. The prostitute eats a 'small pie' (like Sarah in Chapter 36) and Charles becomes 'two people: one who had drunk too much and one who was sexually excited' (p. 316). Her name is sufficient to trigger an 'intolerable spasm' (p. 318) in Charles who has evidently been thinking about Sarah Woodruff. Sarah the prostitute has become what Sarah Woodruff has said so many women who have lost their honour become in great cities.**

Taking it
Further

To research Victorian prostitution visit the 'Victorian London' website at **www.victorianlondon.org** and follow Crime — Prostitution, or visit **www.victorianweb.org/gender/prostitution.html**. If you want a quick overview visit **cai.ucdavis.edu/waters-sites/prostitution/**.

Interesting Pre-Raphaelite artistic representations are *Found* by Rossetti and *The Awakening Conscience* by Holman Hunt. Go to **www.victorianweb.org** then follow the route Visual arts — Painting — Individual artists — Dante Gabriel Rossetti — Paintings — Found; and Visual arts — Painting — Individual artists — William Holman Hunt — Works — The Awakening Conscience — Illustration. Note how the model Rossetti used for *Found* (Fanny Cornforth) bears an uncanny resemblance to Sarah in the novel.

Chapter 41

Sam's bitterness is described. Charles wakes up 'ill but lucid' (p. 320). Sarah, 'as calm a nurse as she had promised to be a prostitute' (p. 321), had helped him while he was sick, going out to hail a cab. In the meantime, her daughter woke up and cried and Charles quietened her with his watch and nursed her. Everywhere in the prostitute's rooms he felt 'not encroaching and hostile objects, but constituting and friendly ones' (p. 323). When the child's mother returned, he handed her the baby and left her five sovereigns. The prostitute followed him to the hansom with 'tears in her eyes' (there is 'no shock to the poor like unearned money', p. 324) and thanked him. Charles told the prostitute 'You are a brave, kind girl' before driving off.

Commentary: **We see Sam's growing antagonism to Charles, who when thinking of the previous night's escapade is 'profoundly relieved' that 'he had not committed the fatal deed' (p. 321) of having sex with someone who might have given him syphilis. He takes some comfort in this strange experience and feels suddenly able to face his future because there are warm feelings in the world which keep hell 'at bay' (p. 323). Fowles sympathises more with Sarah the exploited member of the proletariat than he does with the aristocratic imbeciles Tom and Nat and it is clear that we are to view the two Sarahs as paired characters.**

...we are to view the two Sarahs as paired characters

Chapter 42

Charles apologises to Sam for his behaviour of the night before. Sam brings Charles tea and two letters: one from Grogan, the other evidently from Sarah. Grogan's letter warns Charles to be on his guard as there is a possibility that Sarah might follow him to London. He opens the second letter, finds it contains only an address of three words and burns it, telling Sam to pack for Lyme. Sam informs Charles of his decision to marry Mary and his intention of opening a haberdashery business. Realising that Sam is expecting the money to come from him, Charles says that Sam will only be unhappy if he takes 'ideas above his station' (p. 330). Sam pretends to be shocked and supportive of Charles's new plight. Charles begins to question Sam's loyalty, detecting 'a certain duplicity' (p. 332) in his nature: Sam is indeed duplicitous, as Fowles reveals he had that morning steamed open Sarah's letter.

Commentary: **Perhaps by burning Sarah's note Charles is trying to excise her memory and concentrate on getting back to Ernestina**

in Lyme. He feels that 'Life became a road again' (p. 326) and that he has rediscovered a clear direction. Charles makes an error with Sam by adopting the ancient role of 'infallible master talking to the fallible underling' (p. 330) and dashing Sam's hopes. Also, after deciding he will give Sam the money after receiving Ernestina's dowry ('What would granting Sam his wish matter with Ernestina's money in the bank?', p. 332) he does not tell Sam of his decision. In Marxist terms Sam is beginning to feel that a rebellion is justified and his manoeuvrings to blackmail Charles take on a more serious aspect from now on.

Chapter 43

Charles decides that after his 'night of rebellion' he will 'go through with his marriage' (p. 334). He knows that Sarah's three-word letter of 'Endicott's Family Hotel' is an 'implicit invitation' that 'must be ignored' (p. 334), but on the train journey from London his thoughts turn to a comparison of the two Sarahs and he is able to appreciate Sarah Woodruff's 'uniqueness'. When the train arrives in Exeter he tells Sam they are going to continue directly to Lyme.

Commentary: **Charles feels 'a sense of sadness and of loss' knowing he is about to do what is expected of him, 'the moral, the decent, the correct thing' (p. 335), but in his willingness to accept his fate, he acknowledges his weakness. As he considers Sarah he sees her as a symbol of 'all his lost possibilities' (p. 336) and though Charles remembers her physical and facial features she is still, perhaps, more of an idea to Charles than a real woman. Charles is 'one more ammonite caught in the vast movements of history, stranded now for eternity, a potential turned to a fossil' (p. 336).**

Taking it
Further

An Italian proverb from Boccaccio's *Decameron* is: 'Bocca baciata non perde ventura, anzi rinnova come fa la luna.' (The mouth that has been kissed does not lose its savour; indeed it renews itself just as the moon does.) Why do you think Fowles blends medieval Italian poetry with Pre-Raphaelite art to hint at Sarah's mysterious promise?

Chapter 44

Charles visits Ernestina, who is waiting up, embroidering a blue velvet watch-pocket for him. Charles apologises for not bringing flowers, but Ernestina's mood lightens when he produces an elegant Swiss brooch. The two kiss chastely and Charles begins to reveal his encounters with Sarah, whom he terms 'that miserable female at Marlborough House' (p. 339).

The author claims 'And so ends the story' (p. 340) and provides histories on the main characters. He does not know what happened to Sarah.

Charles and Ernestina marry but do 'not live happily ever after' (p. 340). His uncle Robert has twin sons with Bella Tomkins so Charles has to join Mr Freeman's business. Sam and Mary marry and have children. Grogan and Aunt Tranter both live into their nineties. With obvious relish Fowles reveals that Mrs Poulteney was denied entry into the Heavenly Gates, argued with the 'butler' and 'fell, flouncing and bannering and ballooning, like a shot crow' (p. 341) into Hell.

Commentary: **The epigraph, taken from Clough's poem 'Duty', illustrates that Charles's behaviour is 'the coward's acquiescence' (p. 337). There are a number of unusual stylistic features in the chapter: Charles's and Ernestina's bantering conversation is even more stiltedly artificial than usual ('sweetest', 'dearest', the punning jokes about an 'omnibus-conductor'); the plotting is flimsy and the delivery abrupt. That Charles and Ernestina did not have a particularly happy marriage is believable, but when Fowles says he does not know what happened to Sarah, and says of Sam and Mary 'who can be bothered with the biography of servants?' (p. 340), we know that something is awry, as the novelist has already spent over 300 pages charting the progress of Sarah, Sam and Mary. When we come to the announcement that Charles outlived Ernestina by a decade we are certain that something is badly out of kilter: in Chapter 5 (p. 28) we learn that Ernestina 'died on the day Hitler invaded Poland' (1 September 1939); from Chapter 28 we know that Charles was born on the same day in 1835 that Émile de La Roncière was condemned. If Fowles's plotting in Chapter 44 is to be believed then Charles would have died in 1949, making him 114! The most obvious clue that this (deliberately) badly constructed chapter is not the end of the story lies in the reader's own hands: there are still 120 pages left to read.**

Chapter 45

Fowles admits that he has tricked the reader by having just given a traditional Victorian ending: the last two chapters were all part of Charles's imagination as he was daydreaming on the train. Charles, we learn now, deeply agitated by the three-word letter ('It tormented him, it obsessed him, it confused him', p. 343) chooses to act and not to behave like the 'shabby' version of Charles we saw in Chapter 44. The action restarts when Sam asks Charles if they are to spend the night at Exeter, to which Charles says they will 'put up' at the Ship, and orders Sam to take on the baggage while he 'stretches his legs' (p. 344). After making

some vague claim that he may 'attend Evensong at the Cathedral' Charles sets off in search of Endicott's Family Hotel. Sam, intent on blackmail, decides to follow. After hiring a cab, booking the rooms and laying out Charles's things in seven minutes flat, Sam sets off for Endicott's to spy on Charles. Sam sees Charles arriving but when fifteen minutes pass and it begins to rain Sam bites his nails in 'furious thought' (p. 345) before walking away.

Commentary: **Fowles demonstrates that literature is a construct and the novelist can manipulate characters in any fashion he chooses. This control extends to being able to dupe the reader. Charles, in this new 'real' version of his life, is more decisive: he *chooses* to see Sarah; he wills the act. Sam, similarly, *chooses* to follow Charles. Actions have consequences.**

Chapter 46

In the hotel Charles asks the proprietress for 'Miss Woodruff' and Mrs Endicott informs him that, though Sarah 'turned her ankle something horrible' (p. 347) two days before, he can go up to her room. When Charles enters he sees Sarah sitting by the fire with her feet up, her legs and feet covered by a red Welsh blanket; around her shoulders she wears the green merino shawl from Chapter 36. Beneath that she is wearing only a nightgown and 'her hair was loose and fell over her green shoulders' (p. 348). After some nervous small talk the reader is aware of an intense sexual tension. A little cascade of coals singes Sarah's blanket and when Charles puts out the sparks and replaces the blanket over Sarah's legs, she touches his hand. Swept away on a tide of repressed desire, Charles kisses Sarah with 'an almost savage fierceness' (p. 351), then carries her to the bedroom. He undresses 'wildly' making himself naked except for his long-tailed shirt. He penetrates her and ejaculates almost at once. 'Precisely ninety seconds had passed since he had left her to look in the bedroom' (p. 353).

Commentary: **Fowles again uses Clough for his epigraph, demonstrating how 'the heart still overrules the head' (p. 346) to illustrate the importance of believing that 'in a world of larger scope' what is started we must hope we can complete. Thus Fowles cleverly keeps the idea of completion/incompletion (hinted at symbolically in the unfinished embroidery on the watch-pocket in Chapter 44) before his readers. Sarah has carefully arranged herself for Charles's entrance. When Sarah begins to weep and dabs at her cheek with her handkerchief**

Context

Sarah's looks are based on two of Rossetti's models and mistresses: Jane Morris and Fanny Cornforth. Fanny was a rural blacksmith's daughter originally called Sarah Cox. Fanny moved in with Rossetti as his 'housekeeper' after his wife's death in 1862. Many Rossetti biographers presume Fanny to have been a prostitute before Rossetti met her. See how she represents *possibilities* at **www. settemuse.it**: follow the route Arte/Pittori — R — Rossetti, and click on the picture entitled *Bocca Baciata.*

Charles 'was overcome with a violent sexual desire; a lust a thousand times greater than anything he had felt in the prostitute's room' (p. 350). The reader notices that Sarah's fingers come to rest on her throat. When they kiss Charles struggles to control himself: 'We must not…we must not…this is madness' (p. 351). However, Sarah's response to this is to wrap her arms around him and press his head closer to her neck. Charles carrying Sarah into the bedroom would appear to highlight his dominance yet when he raises her nightgown Sarah opens her legs. That the entire sexual encounter lasts only ninety seconds shows how sexually frustrated Charles is. If this is not premature ejaculation, it is something very close to it. Many Victorians romanticised love, even physical love, as something eternal and spiritual; Fowles tartly undercuts this notion by showing its animalistic nature as well as its unfortunate inclination to brevity. Yet Sarah represents many things to Charles which appear to offer hope of curing his 'long frustration — not merely sexual' (p. 352). Sarah symbolises a 'torrent of things banned, romance, adventure, sin, madness, animality'. Sarah's clothing is fascinating in this chapter. The way Fowles describes her bears a remarkable resemblance to the oil painting *Proserpine* (1882) by Dante Gabriel Rossetti (Birmingham Museum and Art Gallery).

Rossetti describes his painting thus:

> [Proserpine] is represented in a gloomy corridor of her palace, with the fatal fruit in her hand. As she passes, a gleam strikes on the wall behind her from some inlet suddenly opened, and admitting for a moment the sight of the upper world; and she glances furtively towards

Birmingham Museums and Art Gallery/The Bridgeman Art Library

Dante Gabriel Rossetti's painting *Proserpine*

Context

In classical mythology Proserpine, daughter of Ceres, goddess of agriculture and crops, was kidnapped by Pluto, god of the Underworld, to be his wife. She begged to return to earth, but because she had eaten some pomegranate seeds, the food of the dead, Pluto confined her to his kingdom for part of each year. In Rossetti's painting Proserpine holds a pomegranate, which symbolises her captivity and suggests our sexual appetites can have dark, and sometimes deadly, consequences.

it, immersed in thought. The incense-burner stands beside her as the attribute of a goddess. The ivy branch in the background may be taken as a symbol of clinging memory.

Compare this with the way Sarah is described in this chapter:

'Her hair, already enhanced by the green shawl, was ravishingly alive where the firelight touched it…Her fingers…came to rest on her throat…She looked up at him.' (Chapter 46, p. 349)

and earlier:

'An oblique shaft of wan sunlight…found its way through a small rift in the clouds. It lit her face, her figure standing before the entombing greenery behind her; and her face was suddenly very beautiful…full of an inner, as well as outer, light.' (Chapter 18, p. 139)

Chapter 47

Charles was 'paralysed…the radio-activity of guilt crept, crept through his nerves and veins' (p. 354). In the 'distant shadows' he thinks of Ernestina and Mr Freeman. His first utterance is 'I am worse than Varguennes' but Sarah hushes him, saying: 'I cannot think beyond this hour' (p. 355). He continues by saying that he must break his engagement and, even after Sarah tells him that she asks nothing of him and admits she was to blame, he behaves like a typical Victorian man, speaking of 'obligations'. When she declares her love for him, Charles is touched, believing society has been wrong about the 'French Lieutenant's Woman'. As he is dressing, noticing the bloodstains on the front tails of his shirt, he realises that Sarah was a virgin. Sarah, who has no sprained ankle, admits her virginity but can give no definite reasons for any of her many lies. She says that she did follow Varguennes to Weymouth, but, as he was with a prostitute, she returned to the Talbots. Charles is bewildered when Sarah says she cannot marry him and orders him to leave her alone. Hurt by her formality, Charles leaves.

Commentary: **Ideas of duty and obligation still control Charles, who misses the clues Sarah gives him: she was 'to blame' and when they had sex she 'wished it so' (p. 355). In this moment, Charles idealises Sarah: he sees her as mysterious, 'strange' but well-intentioned. He sees her behaviour as a 'sacrifice' (p. 356)** and not as a choice. So he Victorianises her as an idealised, pure woman but when he notices the bloodstain, its implications horrify him. From idealising her purity, he careers straight into the opposite opinion that she is a predatory, whore-like seductress. When questioned, Sarah adopts the old defiance of her Lyme days, admitting her virginity, acknowledging her deception but claiming 'I shall not trouble you again' (p. 358). She claims she loves Charles but her language becomes melodramatic: 'I beseech you. Leave!' (p. 359). By now many readers may well be as confused and bewildered as Charles at Sarah's behaviour but Fowles has been careful to make her understandable at least from a modern vantage point. Sarah wanted sex with Charles, arranged a venue for it to happen, invited him, seduced him by making herself appear small and vulnerable via the trickery of the bandage, lit a romantic fire to show off her lustrous hair in the best light, enhanced her natural beauty with the green merino shawl, ensured she was naked under her new nightgown, touched his hand when it rested on her leg, drew him into a more passionate embrace when he wanted to break away, returned his passionate kisses with equal ardour, arranged herself on the bed for him, parted her legs when he lifted up her nightgown and threw her arms around him 'as if she would bind him to her for...eternity' (p. 353) as he ejaculated inside her. Charles 'like many Victorian men...could not really believe that any woman of refined sensibilities could enjoy being a receptacle for male lust' (p. 356). In this belief he is again a 'poor fossil'.

> **Pause for *Thought***
>
> There is an Italian sonnet in the top right-hand corner of Rossetti's painting; lines 9 to 11 can be translated:
>
> *Afar from mine own self I seem, and wing Strange ways in thought, and listen for a sign: And still some heart unto some soul doth pine*
>
> In what ways might these words suggest Sarah's ambiguous position in Victorian society ('afar from mine own self'), inscrutably demonstrating 'strange ways in thought'?

Chapter 48

Charles leaves Endicott's and, feeling the 'need for sanctuary' (p. 360) he enters a small church where the curate is about to lock up. He allows Charles to remain, asking him to return the church keys to his house when he is finished. Wanting to purge his guilt, he stares at the crucifix 'but instead of Christ's face, he saw only Sarah's' (p. 362). Realising that 'it was hopeless' and knowing that his prayer is not heard, he begins 'abruptly to cry' before beginning a dialogue 'between his better and his worse self' (p. 363) or perhaps with the crucifix. Charles experiences an illuminating insight that freedom involves the relinquishing of organised Christianity and believing that his new life must contain Sarah; he says a brief prayer and leaves the Church.

In Giovanni Guareschi's stories of postwar Italy, the Catholic priest Don Camillo and the Communist mayor Peppone are arch-rivals. Don Camillo hears the voice of Christ through the crucifix in his church and is often gently rebuked for his impatience and occasional outbursts of bad-tempered violence. The Voice recommends tolerance and tries to teach Don Camillo a wisdom his religious enthusiasms do not easily allow him to see. Through this plot device, conservative institutions are humorously and charmingly chided.

Commentary: **Not only does Fowles engage ideas about religion and Existentialist freedom but also inserts a most unusual and new technique to the novel to communicate Charles's indecision to the reader. This technique is the dialogue (or internal monologue) with the crucifix. Though new in the context of this novel, a man having a conversation with a crucifix is not new to European literature and Fowles owes a debt of gratitude to Italian novelist Giovanni Guareschi and his *Don Camillo* stories.**

Charles experiences a genuine moment of awareness when he decides he wants to choose Sarah and to turn his back on many Victorian beliefs that have baulked his progress (duty, honour, Christianity, obligation) and that have made him 'a fossil' who had 'become, while still alive, as if dead' (p. 366). Yet he has not evolved fully: he still has to 'uncrucify' himself from Sarah. Fowles communicates that Charles has not quite developed an Existential awareness in his prayer to a God he no longer believes in and who he knew did not listen.

Chapter 49

Charles returns the church keys to the curate, who invites him to confession. Charles refuses, able to take 'heart in his own new vision… shriven of established religion for the rest of his life' (p. 370). Fowles digresses to inform the reader that though a modern man would go straight back to Sarah, Charles's next step is to go to his lodgings where he washes his bloodstained shirt before Sam can see it, and writes a conventional love-letter to Sarah informing her of the 'necessity…to terminate' his engagement. The letter takes several drafts and Charles decides it is too late to send it that night so the next morning orders Sam to take the letter and a small packet to Sarah and to bring back a reply, if any. When Sam returns without a reply, Charles assumes that Sarah, by accepting the gift of the same Swiss brooch we saw in Chapter 44, has accepted both his apology and his marriage proposal.

Commentary: **That Charles is a changed man is clear when he rejects the offer of confession from the 'shrimp' of a curate, but that the evolution has only just begun is conveyed via his 'accursed sense of Duty and Propriety', which 'stood like castle walls' (p. 371) against him going straight back to Sarah. He does not take personal responsibility for delivering the life-changing love-letter, relying on Sam to do it for him. The reader is by now highly suspicious of Sam and may infer that the non-appearance** of a reply from Sarah might be due to Sam's non-delivery of the letter and its accompanying package.

Chapter 50

Charles tells Ernestina of his decision to break off the engagement, at first claiming that he is 'not worthy' of her, before acknowledging that part of his regard was ignobly based on her financial fortune and admitting that there is another woman. Ernestina self-consciously and dramatically collapses to the floor, but Charles realises that this is a contrived movement and leaves the room, promising to send Dr Grogan round.

Commentary: **Fowles's epigraph from *The Origin of Species* is playful: the reader must decide whether Charles is one of the fitter specimens of his species marked down for survival by natural selection or one of the life forms which will become rarer and finally extinct. Ernestina's reaction to Charles's shocking news is initially quite typical of many fictional Victorian women: she blames herself for her faults and promises to change, but the reader then sees a vicious side to Ernestina when she thinks it is her inferior social status Charles finds unappealing. She turns on him with considerable vitriol, threatening both suicide and her father dragging Charles's name 'through the mire' (p. 386). Shallow though she is, the reader perhaps feels it difficult to be too harsh on Ernestina: like most women of her class she is desperate to conform and other than being herself she has actually done nothing wrong. Her position in society has been jeopardised by Charles's decision. Her pain and misery are genuine enough — despite the histrionic 'faint'.**

Chapter 51

Charles tells the shocked Grogan about the broken engagement, and the doctor guesses that Charles has abandoned Ernestina because of Sarah. Tacitly promising not to mention Sarah's name to Ernestina, he goes to Aunt Tranter's house. Charles returns to his hotel but is interrupted by Sam, who has heard of the end of the engagement from Mary. After bringing Charles the brandy he orders, Sam questions Charles further about his intentions and where he intends to live. Angered and in no mood to talk, Charles shouts at Sam, who responds in kind, declaring he is leaving Charles's employment. Sam is rude as he leaves but Fowles

Taking it Further ▶

At www.youtube.com listen to the Peter Gabriel song 'Solsbury Hill' (search for Peter Gabriel Solsbury Hill); the lyrics are available at www.lyricsfreak.com via P — Peter Gabriel lyrics — Solsbury Hill. The clip from a Peter Gabriel concert shows the artist cycling round the circular stage. Why do you think the motif of travelling is so important to musicians like Gabriel and writers like Fowles to capture the sense of escape from the 'machinery' of enslavement?

Task 2

We have already seen that Ernestina keeps a diary. Write her diary entry after Charles has broken off his engagement, giving her thoughts and feelings about not only the painful meeting itself but also her engagement to Charles in general, trying to recreate the authentic voice which Fowles constructs for Ernestina.

cryptically tells the reader that Sam knows he is guilty of a crime even bigger than mutiny. Meanwhile, Charles questions the sanity of his actions, wondering if he should rush back to Ernestina and beg forgiveness, but an image of Sarah's face 'gentle, acquiescent…soft' (p. 391) stops him. While he is writing a letter to Mr Freeman, Grogan arrives.

Commentary: **The argument between Charles and Sam that has been brewing since Chapter 26 is meant to be understood in relation to the epigraph from Matthew Arnold's *Culture and Anarchy* (1869). Sam is a modern working-class man who unlike the many generations of working people who have lived before him is no longer happy to be deferential to those above him in the social hierarchy. He is 'beginning to assert…threaten… smash' (p. 388). Arnold fears the resultant anarchy but Fowles presents it as a consequence of social conditioning, a kind of inevitable evolutionary development. Charles's mistake is essentially the same mistake he has been making over and over again: because Sam is a servant Charles treats him (in the words of Aristotle) as 'a tool with life in it', dismissible and inconsequential. However, his love for Sarah appears to be genuine: the vision of her face 'gentle, acquiescent…soft' prevents him from rushing back to Ernestina.**

Chapter 52

Grogan tells the bewildered Aunt Tranter to 'humour' Ernestina and watch her day and night for a couple of days, assuring her that Ernestina will be 'as gay as a linnet' (p. 393) in six months. Grogan promises to see Charles and 'have his hide for this' (p. 394). Mary tells Mrs Tranter of Sam's dismissal from his job. After ascertaining that Mary truly loves Sam, Mrs Tranter promises that she will find him a post. Mary happily runs outside into 'Sam's anxious but eager arms' (p. 396).

Commentary: **Mrs Tranter displays mixed feelings about Charles: one moment refusing to believe he is capable of such betrayal, the next raging that he should be 'whipped and put in the stocks' (p. 394). Mrs Tranter's confusion illustrates a key ingredient in Victorian society — Charles with complete success acted the part of the perfect Victorian gentleman while simultaneously hiding a more disturbing, darker side. Mary's distress now that Sam is unemployed illustrates that without the say-so of someone further up the social hierarchy the working** classes are essentially trapped, unable to make their own decisions: this economic dependency is both restricting and demeaning. Aunt Tranter's kindness is genuine but she does look on Mary and Sam as members of 'the deserving poor'.

Chapter 53

Grogan demands an explanation for Charles's behaviour with Sarah and is given the entire tale. The doctor reprimands Charles by saying 'a gentleman remains a gentleman when he rejects advice' (p. 398) but that he does not remain one when he lies. Charles counters the insult by saying that he does not want to live 'a lifetime of pretence' by marrying Ernestina. Grogan is concerned that Charles's quest for self-knowledge has embroiled an innocent girl in a catastrophic situation for which she is not responsible. Grogan warns Charles that he may still have misunderstood Sarah, who could easily be deranged, and gives Charles the benefit of his wisdom: he knows that Charles (like Grogan himself) wishes to belong to a rational and scientific elect and argues that only when that elect have introduced 'a finer and fairer morality into this dark world' (p. 401) can they be considered as superior or deserving. As Grogan leaves he shakes Charles's hand and wishes him well but with a 'glint in his eyes' he warns Charles that if he has not left Lyme within the hour he will be back with the 'largest horsewhip I can find' (p. 401). Charles bows his assent and closes the door.

Commentary: **Grogan delivers a kind of sermon after Charles's 'confession', the consequence of which is that Charles has his first taste of being ostracised from society. The reader realises he is now like Sarah when we first met her: he is an outcast and must live with the consequences of his decision to free himself from convention. A detailed analysis of the language of Chapter 53 is given in the *Working with the text* section of this guide (pp. 87–90).**

Chapter 54

Before leaving Lyme Charles tries to find Sam but is unable to locate him. Sensing that he will be at Mrs Tranter's, Charles takes a cab to Exeter and gradually his spirits rise: 'among the rich green fields and May hedgerows…it was difficult not to see the future as fertile — a new life lay ahead of him' (p. 402). He knows that he and Sarah 'were not yet carved into…harmony' but believed they 'were of the same stone'

Pause for *Thought*

Fowles claims that R. L. Stevenson's novella *The Strange Case of Dr Jekyll and Mr Hyde* is 'the best guidebook to the age…Behind its latterday Gothick lies a very profound and epoch-revealing truth' (p. 372): 'Every Victorian had two minds…[This] is the one piece of equipment we must always take with us on our travels back to the nineteenth century' (p. 371). How has Fowles revealed that Charles has at least 'two minds' up to now in the novel?

(p. 403). It is night by the time he reaches Endicott's. When he arrives, he confidently tells Mrs Endicott that Sarah expects him, only to learn that Sarah has left for London that morning and has left no address or note. Stunned, Charles leaves his card and tells Mrs Endicott to get in touch with him 'without fail' if she hears anything. He asks her if a manservant had been there that morning with a letter and package for Sarah. Neither Mrs Endicott nor Betty Anne the servant has any knowledge of Sam and the letter. Sam's betrayal infuriates Charles, who is tempted to go to the police but realises that this will not bring Sarah back. Charles's only 'light in the gloom' (p. 405) is that Sarah is somewhere in London. That night he kneels by his bed and prays that he will find her, even if it takes the rest of his life.

Commentary: **In Charles's mind Sarah has always represented the freedom represented by travel, so when he fantasises about his new life with Sarah he sees her in a variety of increasingly exotic locations: 'The Alhambra! Moonlight, the distant sound below of singing gypsies, such grateful, tender eyes…' (p. 403). It is therefore bitterly ironic that upon his return to Exeter, Charles discovers that Sarah has indeed gone travelling but without him and he has no way of finding out exactly where she has gone. When Charles learns of Sam's betrayal, everything makes sense. He understands Sam's reasons for suddenly leaving his employment and running to Aunt Tranter's: Sam had read the letter and kept the brooch. Though now Charles is in many ways Existentially free — symbolised by his final but lonely escape from the petty provincial values of Lyme — the novelist shows that an air of Victorian irrationality lingers about him as he kneels and prays to a God he does not really believe in for the second time since his epiphany in Chapter 48. The careful reader will notice the futility of the act as much as the deep devotion to Sarah that it reveals.**

Task 3

How does the novel present ideas about two different sorts of freedom: the freedom *from* and the freedom *to*? Which sort of freedom do you think Fowles considers to be the more important and why?

Chapter 55

The next morning Charles boards the London train. So much does he crave solitude that whenever anyone looks into Charles's compartment he glowers at them with a 'Gorgon stare' (p. 406) and they move away. However, just as the train is pulling out a bearded stranger enters the compartment. Charles decides to ignore the 'unpleasant' stranger, who reciprocates the snub. Charles begins working out the permutations of how he may find Sarah but falls asleep. His fellow-traveller eyes Charles and Fowles informs us that it is he himself gazing at Charles, wondering

'Now what could I do with you?' (p. 408). The novelist reveals that he has already thought of ending Charles's career here, leaving him for eternity on his way to London, but the conventions of Victorian fiction do not allow for an open, inconclusive ending. Fowles claims that though it is very clear what Charles wants it is not at all clear what his 'protagonist' (Sarah) wants. Since Fowles believes in the freedom of his characters he does not want to 'fix the fight', so concludes that his only solution is to give two versions of the novel's ending. Then his only dilemma is that he cannot give both versions at once so to determine which ending he should save for the final, 'real version' (p. 409) he takes out a florin and spins it. Charles wakes from his sleep and the train pulls into Paddington. As Charles summons a porter the bearded stranger disappears into the throng.

Commentary: **Inserting the novelist as a character into his own novel is a highly unusual technique and was a brave literary experiment in 1969. Fowles has obvious fun at his own expense, comparing himself to a butler, a lay-preacher and even someone considering a 'devious sexual approach' (p. 408). Under the novelist's jocular self-deprecation Fowles wants the reader to see these two endings as being equally possible and true, though one may seem more contrived than the other due to the 'tyranny of the last chapter' (p. 409), which will always appear to be the author's final judgement.**

Chapter 56

Three weeks have passed since Sarah's disappearance; Charles has hired four detectives to find Sarah but after exhaustive searches she cannot be traced. Charles receives a letter from Mr Freeman's solicitors summoning him to a meeting which is deeply humiliating for Charles, who learns that his liaison with Sarah is known via an informant's tip-off (undoubtedly Sam's). Consequently Charles is forced to sign a *confessio delicti* in which he admits to having broken his engagement to Ernestina due to his 'own criminal selfishness and faithlessness' (p. 416). His 'clandestine liaison' with Miss Woodruff proves that his conduct was 'dishonourable' and that he has 'forever forfeited the right to be considered a gentleman' (p. 417). In the days following, Charles withdraws from all society apart from Montague's and throws himself into his search for Sarah, which is still unfruitful. By the end of June he stops searching altogether and Montague tells him he is wasting his time: Sarah's motive was 'vindictive destruction' (p. 420) and Grogan had been right about

Context

'*Confessio delicti*' is Latin for 'confession of the crime'. Breach of promise cases for broken engagements were common in the Victorian courts and were only rendered obsolete by an Act of Parliament which became law in 1971.

Taking it Further

Fowles spends a lot of time in the novel writing about the importance to Charles of travelling. Listen to the Bob Dylan song 'Tangled Up In Blue' available at www.youtube.com (search for Dylan Tangled Blue) and read the (slightly altered) lyrics at www.songmeanings.net via B — Bob Dylan — Tangled Up In Blue. What differences and similarities can you find in the outlook and lives of the narrator of 'Tangled Up In Blue' and Charles up to this point in the novel?

Sarah all along. When Montague proves that Sarah has not died because no death has been recorded Charles 'abruptly, one evening' decides to go abroad.

Commentary: **In Existentialist terms, Charles is realising the painful cost of his freedom from Ernestina. The contents of the *confessio delicti* demonstrate the contractual nature of marriage, showing that for many Victorians, economic and social concerns were more important than love. Freeman will show the document to any prospective father-in-law, so in effect Charles will not be able to take a wife in England. Charles appears finally to admit defeat over Sarah, and in his depressed state seems to think that either she no longer cares for him or even that she never cared for him. With nothing to keep him in England, he decides to travel.**

Chapter 57

It is now February 1869. The setting is Chelsea embankment and we are introduced to the pregnant Mary strolling by the Thames. She sees Sarah getting out of a cab and entering a well-to-do house. Later in their modest marital home Mary tells her news to Sam, who has kept secret that he did not deliver Charles's letter and kept the brooch, which he subsequently gave to Mary as a present. Sam's and Mary's life over the last twenty months is described: they already have one daughter; and due to services rendered by Sam in supplying Sarah's name for the *confessio delicti* he got a job in Freeman's store. A hard worker and gifted window-dresser ('Freeman's for Choice') Sam has climbed the social ladder to the point where he is earning over thirty shillings a week; yet his conscience troubles him. Mary's new life is a marvellous dream: she now has a house which costs nineteen pounds a year to rent and a maid. The chapter concludes with Sam and Mary staring at the purloined brooch, 'the emblem of their good fortune' (p. 427), which the novelist tells us is thoroughly deserved in Mary's case, but 'now finally to be paid for, in his'.

Commentary: **The beginning of spring suggests that various changes for the better may be about to occur but things are not necessarily going to go perfectly, as traces of winter snow are still visible. A symbol of this partial fulfilment is Sam's new job at Freeman's: it is paid employment but not his own haberdashery business. The frequent mentions of money show** that though Sam has made considerable financial improvements in his life since he left Charles's service he has merely known the price of everything but the value of nothing. That his conscience is now troubling him and that he is resolved to make some kind of amends shows that at heart he is not a vindictive man. The brooch has been associated with all three women up to now: we saw Charles give it to Ernestina in the 'imaginary' ending in Chapter 44; it was intended for Sarah in Chapter 49 and now resides on Mary's breast.

Chapter 58

Charles's lonely travels are described. Palaeontology no longer interests him but literature occupies him and he forms an attachment to Tennyson, keeping a copy of *Maud* with him constantly. When he has sex it is with mute cynicism: 'Love had left the world' (p. 432). The search for Sarah is conducted by Montague and comprises 'advertisements in the London newspapers' (p. 431). Charles's uncle now has a son and after sending a letter of congratulation Charles decided never to set foot in Winsyatt again. Sometimes Charles imagines Sarah beside him but he becomes 'increasingly unsure of the frontier between the real Sarah and the Sarah he had created in so many… dreams' (p. 432). Charles meets two Philadelphians in Paris who awake a responsive chord in him. With his curiosity aroused Charles decides to visit America.

Commentary: **The philosophical importance of Matthew Arnold's *To Marguerite* (p. 430) is vital. Fowles cleverly juxtaposes the brilliant *Marguerite* with Charles's own poor stab at explaining his loneliness in verse. Fowles loves the poem because it beautifully describes Existentialist anxiety ninety years before Sartre's work: 'We mortal millions live alone' but because aeons ago 'we were parts of a single continent' we feel a 'longing like despair' for connection. 'A God' has ordered that the unity be broken and that between the 'shores' (geological, geopolitical but most importantly human) there is the barrier of 'the unplumb'd, salt, estranging sea'. Charles is of course about to cross the sea and the space between him and Sarah will be an entire continent and an estranging ocean. America is important as a symbol of (r)evolutionary development: 'one day America might supersede the older species' (p. 433).**

Context

In many ancient cultures the oyster shell in which the pearl grows is associated with the female genitalia, and thus the pearl is an emblem of fecundity. Coral, a natural organic substance, was said to cure madness and give wisdom. It is clear via the symbolism of the brooch that it was an entirely inappropriate gift for Ernestina and though it looks well on Mary, it would have been a more appropriate gift for the 'wild' Sarah.

Context

Henry James (1843–1916) is 'the master' Fowles will not ape (p. 436). The American James became a British citizen in 1915. Fowles admired James's technique of writing from the point of view of his characters to explore issues of consciousness and perception as well as James's insistence that writers be allowed the freedom to present their view of the world.

Context

In Greek mythology, the Sphinx asked travellers a riddle to allow them entry to Thebes: 'Which creature in the morning goes on four legs, at midday on two, and in the evening upon three, and the more legs it has, the weaker it is?' She killed anyone unable to answer. When Oedipus answered 'Man — who crawls on all fours as a baby, walks on two feet as an adult, and uses a walking stick in old age', she killed herself.

Chapter 59

Charles finds America delightful. Once or twice he could have 'easily lost his heart' but memories of the *confessio delicti* 'stood between him and every innocent girl's face he saw' (p. 437); only Sarah's face could 'forgive and exorcize' that document. Many American women remind him of Sarah and the more time he spends in the USA the more his old image of Sarah as a remarkable woman is revived. He advertises for her wherever he goes. America reawakens Charles's faith in freedom and, empathising with the American people's need for independence, he considers emigrating. Meanwhile, Sam has anonymously informed Montague of Sarah's address and the solicitor has cabled 'SHE IS FOUND. LONDON. MONTAGUE' (p. 440). Charles's eyes 'smart with tears' and he makes arrangements for his immediate return.

Commentary: **Charles's American experiences have refreshed and enlivened him. He is now liberated but the careful reader will note that as soon as he hears that Sarah has been found he finds the allure of her mystery irresistible.**

Chapter 60

It is 31 May 1869. Montague has informed Charles that the only clue on the anonymous letter was the London postmark and the copperplate handwriting. Charles knows this is not Sarah's but does not recognise the hand of Sam in the enterprise. Montague had arranged for a surveillance of Sarah, now living as 'Mrs Roughwood'. Despite the title Sarah is not married. Against Montague's advice Charles explains that he must see the Sphinx-like Sarah because she haunts him still.

When Charles arrives at the house 'his new American self' is swept away and he is 'conscious of being a gentleman about to call on a superior form of servant' (p. 443). A girl answers the door, and Charles asks to see Sarah. A man enters the hall and gives permission for Charles to meet Sarah. Charles notices many art works and is able to recognise the art-school to which most of them belonged, scandalous and shocking twenty years ago but now highly collectable and valuable. Charles, believing he is in the house of an art collector, asks the girl if Sarah works as a governess, to be told with 'amused surprise' (p. 445) that Sarah is no longer in that position.

Charles is asked to wait and from his vantage point he can see into a room where two men are admiring a painting. Stunned, Charles recognises one of the men as a very notable figure in the art world and begins to piece in the clues: 'the man downstairs! Those paintings and drawings!…He saw nothing; but only the folly of his own assumption that fallen women must continue falling' (p. 445). Then he hears a sound as Sarah enters the room. She is now dressed in brilliant clothing, 'flagrantly rejecting all formal contemporary notions of female fashion' (p. 446); looking two years younger she is both 'electric and bohemian' and reminds Charles of the American women he found so attractive.

Sarah seems surprised to see Charles and claims not to know that Charles had broken his engagement, admitting 'Life has been kind to me' (p. 447). Charles ascertains the identity of the man he has just recognised and the identity of the artist whose house this is and Sarah leads him up some stairs into an artist's studio. Fowles gives clues about the artist's identity from one of the paintings he describes: 'a barely begun oil…a hint of a young woman looking sadly down, foliage sketched faint behind the head' (p. 447). The careful reader will remember this is how Sarah was described in Chapters 18 and 46. Sarah tells Charles that she is the artist's amanuensis. Charles wishes he could ask her how she had met the artist, on what terms they lived, but 'the room divided them. All divided them' (p. 448).

He presses on with his nervous questioning and learns that Sarah passes as a widow, that the artist's wife is dead 'but not in his heart' (p. 449), that he shares the house with his sister and brother and a 'notoriously disreputable' poet. Charles, unnerved by the revelations, imagines 'some orgiastic *ménage à quatre — à cinq*' going on. He also recalls gossip of the artist's alleged opium addiction but cannot reconcile the presence of the widely respected critic in such 'a den of iniquity' (p. 449). Charles struggles to allow his better self to dismiss his suspicions yet he does so and quietly though formally tells Sarah what happened that night in Exeter when he decided to forsake Ernestina because of Sarah. 'Sam's gross betrayal' is explained. Sarah and Charles have a detailed conversation, which ends when Sarah leaves the room, promising that 'a lady in this house' will explain her 'real nature' (p. 457). A detailed analysis of this section of the novel can be found in the *Form, structure and language* section of this guide, pp. 61–62.

The girl who first opened the door to Charles returns with a little girl whom she sets down on the carpet. Charles, assuming he is waiting for a lady, enquires when she will come. 'She is come,' says the girl before leaving. Charles scans the baby's 'small face like some archaeologist who has just unearthed the first example of a lost ancient script' (p. 460), gets out his watch for the baby and sits her on his knee 'intent on her face,

Pause for *Thought*

Charles is one of the most well-travelled characters in literary history and Sarah is clearly identified as a creature with huge destructive power, but the myth has another resonance. The outcome of trying to answer the riddle is an *either/or*: either the Sphinx survives and the traveller dies, or vice versa. How far do you agree that Fowles is suggesting that Montague is unable to see a happy outcome that will unite Charles and Sarah?

Pause for *Thought*

By choosing not to inform us who these people are it could be argued that Fowles is building up suspense and enhancing reader, enjoyment, but an alternative view is that it alienates the reader, who, approaching the climax of the novel and desperate for information (we have not met Sarah since Chapter 47), finds such Postmodern tinkering irksome. What is your view of this?

her hands, her every inch. And on every word that had been spoken in that room'.

Sarah enters and takes her baby into her arms. The baby is Sarah's and Charles's: Rossetti (the identity finally revealed) had approached the pregnant Sarah on the street and had asked to be allowed to draw her. She agreed and he looked after her, even suggesting the baby's name, Lalage (which Charles feels obliged to inform Sarah is from the Greek *lalageo*: 'to babble like a brook', p. 461). Rossetti is the child's godfather. Sarah acknowledges that this history is strange and Charles, overwhelmed and 'numbed', struggles to understand her behaviour. Enigmatic now as ever, Sarah tells Charles 'It had to be so' (p. 462). Fowles tells us that Charles understands now: 'it had been in God's hands, in His forgiveness of their sins'. When Charles asks about her cruel words she replies they 'had to be spoken'. Charles asks 'Shall I ever understand your parables?' (p. 462) before kissing her auburn hair. The last activity described is Lalage banging her doll against her father Charles's cheek.

Commentary: **Charles does not detect Montague's reticence or his belief that things will go badly. Montague evidently knows from his clerk that the house is Rossetti's and assumes Sarah is the artist's mistress. Montague perhaps foresees danger when he compares Sarah to the Sphinx.**

Fowles teases us about the identities of the artist, the famous critic and the 'libidinous' poet currently living under the artist's roof. It is not until p. 459 that Fowles admits we are in Rossetti's house, which he shares with his sister Christina and his brother William. The resident poet is Charles Algernon Swinburne, whose *Poems and Ballads* (1866) was attacked so viciously on the grounds of indecency and anti-Christianity that Swinburne was very nearly subjected to criminal prosecution. Swinburne was vilified by John Morley as 'the libidinous laureate of a pack of satyrs'. The critic is John Ruskin, a staunch supporter of the Pre-Raphaelites and, among other things, the man who coined the phrase 'pathetic fallacy' to describe the ascription of human emotions to impersonal natural forces.

Charles, caught between his new American self and his old conventional self, is clearly uncomfortable; Sarah remains mysterious, claiming to be unaware of the advertisements and broken engagement but later admitting that she knew everything six months after leaving Exeter. She admits she had 'thrown' herself at him, forced herself upon him, saying: 'A madness was

in me at that time' (p. 451). This proved, at least partially, that Grogan's diagnosis was accurate. (For more information on this see *Form, structure and language*, the section on p. 61 of this guide beginning with the quotation 'Language is like shot-silk; so much depends on the angle at which it is held.')

A convention of Victorian romance is a happy ending and in one sense that is what Chapter 60 gives us, with the nuclear family of Charles, Sarah and Lalage looking towards some sort of future together. However, as we have seen with Chapter 44, Chapter 60 contains a number of jarring elements placed by Fowles deliberately to stretch his readers' sense of credulity about plot and character.

For many readers it does not quite ring true that Charles, evolved and free from religion for twenty months, would see Sarah's cruelty as a 'judgement' from God about the forgiveness of 'sins', the definition of which he no longer found authentic. Similarly, it jars that he would choose the noun 'parables' (p. 462) as a metaphor for Sarah's account of her conduct, thus fixing his understanding to a Christianised world-view he firmly rejected in Chapter 49. The ending with its references to poorly executed music — 'a thousand violins cloy very rapidly without percussion' (p. 463) — presents another clue that though hyperbole is a feature of much Victorian literature, there has been a good deal of melodramatic over-orchestration in this chapter and the careful reader will realise that there is something inauthentic about it. This ending, in fact, represents Charles's analysis of Christina Rossetti's verse, which features 'a certain incomprehensible mysticism…a passionate obscurity' and which is 'rather absurdly muddled over the frontiers of human and divine love' (p. 459), which is why Fowles gives us his third and final ending of *The French Lieutenant's Woman* in Chapter 61.

> **Pause for *Thought***
>
> The reader may well question the believability of Charles's and Sarah's only sexual encounter apparently resulting in a pregnancy. However, such coincidences are features of many Victorian novels, not all of them bad ones; it happens to Hardy's Tess in *Tess of the d'Urbervilles*, for example. How do you respond to Fowles's use of this plot device here?

Chapter 61

For the third and final time in the novel, the author inserts himself into the narrative as an 'extremely important-looking person', though now rather 'foppish and Frenchified' (p. 464), who observes 16 Cheyne Walk, Rossetti's house. He takes out a watch and turns it back fifteen minutes before summoning his waiting landau and leaving. The narration returns to the point of Charles's melodramatic words of Chapter 60: 'No. It is

as I say. You have not only planted the dagger in my breast, you have delighted in twisting it' (p. 466). However, following Charles's outburst (described as 'tragic' in Chapter 60): 'if there is justice in heaven — your punishment shall outlast eternity' (p. 466), Sarah does not block his march to the door with the words 'I cannot let you go believing that' but cries the far more formal 'Mr Smithson!' reminding the reader of the Sarah we saw ordering Charles out of her room at Endicott's in Chapter 47.

Charles tells Sarah that she is 'selfish and bigoted' and even Mrs Poulteney is a saint compared to her. Sarah counters that it would be selfish to marry Charles knowing that she could not love him as a wife must and Charles gives her a 'freezing look'. Once again Sarah calls out 'Mr Smithson!' When he looks at her he is shocked to see 'in her eyes…a suggestion of a smile' (p. 467) reminiscent of the one she had given him the day 'they were nearly surprised by Sam and Mary'. Her body language seems to be saying 'Look, can you not see, a solution exists?' He realises that he is being offered a Platonic relationship which may one day become more intimate and is 'for a moment tempted' to accept her offer but resists, believing 'he would become the secret butt of this corrupt house…the pet donkey' (p. 468). He sees his own true superiority to her: 'She could give only to possess…From the first she had manipulated him. She would do so to the end.' With this realisation, Charles throws Sarah 'one last burning look of rejection' and, holding back the tears, passes the girl who had shown him up 'holding a small child in her arms' (p. 468). She opens her mouth to speak but Charles silences her with a 'wild yet icy look'. He leaves the house with his belief in himself as 'the last honourable man on the way to the scaffold' (p. 468) intact. He has now found 'an atom of faith in himself, a true uniqueness, on which to build' (p. 470). The novel ends with Fowles telling the reader that Charles has understood that life is to be 'endured'.

Commentary: **The novelist who appears in the beginning of the final chapter has found something laughable in the events of Chapter 60, and sets back the clock so there can be a different outcome. Cynicism is a feature of much Existential literature. Sarah offers no excuses for her behaviour and in this version she chooses to say nothing, though her attempt to restrain Charles by laying her hand on his arm may be interpreted as an implicit offer of a relationship, but a relationship entirely on her terms and a relationship that would not involve marriage, accommodating Sarah's bohemian new life. This scenario, in Charles's analysis, would give Sarah all the power in any subsequent relationship: ' "Power" seems always fascistic,**

Task **4**

Read Christina Rossetti's poem *Goblin Market*, which, among other things, contains the themes of Adam and Eve, Forbidden Fruit, Temptation, Love and Sacrifice. How far do you agree with Charles's critique of her verse (p. 459)? What links can you find between *Goblin Market* and the endings Fowles gives us in Chapters 60 and 61?

potentially. It always kills true thought and feeling. That is why individual action and at least seeming free will are so important' (Fowles's interview with Diane Vipond, 1995). Charles exercises his own free will when he leaves Rossetti's house.

In this version of the ending it is not even clear whether the baby is indeed Sarah's, as she 'has remained in the studio, staring down at the garden below, at a child and a young woman, the child's mother perhaps, who sit on the grass engaged in making a daisy-chain' (p. 469). Clearly there is a baby in the house who is not Sarah's. Are there two babies of roughly the same age but with different mothers living in Rossetti's household in May 1869? In Fowles's world there appear to be no absolute definites, just unending series of potentials: in the novelist's own words again, 'Everything is relative. No absolute, except our… final ignorance. We may pretend we know, but we never do.' The novelist tells the reader that it is imperative not to think that this is 'a less plausible ending' (p. 469) to Charles's and Sarah's story than the events of Chapter 60.

The extract on p. 464 from Martin Gardner's *The Ambidextrous Universe* (1967) defining the co-operation between 'chance' and 'natural law' is hugely important to Charles's situation before the 'final' ending, which Fowles uses to expound his Existentialist philosophy. There is no god to intervene in human life, which is best explained in the definition by Karl Marx as *'the actions of men* (and of women) *in pursuit of their ends'* (p. 469).

We make our lives within our 'hazard-given abilities', which idea takes us back to a recurring theme in Fowles's work: the importance of hazard (chance) within life. To be free is to make the best possible humane choice under whatever circumstances apply at the time. Fowles referred to this decision-making moment as 'the fork in the road' that Charles reaches in Chapter 61; by choosing to be free of Sarah he makes himself free. He now has principles which guide him and has discovered that true piety is 'acting what one knows' (Matthew Arnold, *Notebooks*, 1868). The novelist tells us that he believes Sarah's behaviour has always been guided by this fundamental principle, 'though a modern Existentialist would no doubt substitute "humanity" or "authenticity" for "piety"'. (p. 469) Charles will endure his life a wiser and freer man, and 'return to America' — in the words of Matthew Arnold, which we first heard in Chapter 58 — across 'the unplumb'd, salt, estranging sea.'

Themes

Fowles claimed that the novel's overarching theme was freedom and how to achieve it, so it is a good idea to see each of the following headings as individual threads in a wider debate about freedom.

Feminism

On 31 March 1776, Mrs Abigail Adams of Braintree, Massachusetts, wrote a letter to her husband John, later the second President of the United States. He was attending the Philadelphia Congress, the business of which was to decide whether the American colonies broke away from England or remained loyal to the Crown. There was never much doubt about the outcome. Abigail wrote, 'I long to hear that you have declared an independency…and in the new Code of Laws which I suppose it will be necessary for you to make, I desire you would *Remember the Ladies*, and be more generous and favourable to them than your ancestors. Do not put such unlimited power into the hands of Husbands.'

John Adams did not stand up for women's rights at the Philadelphia Congress and neither did any of the other men present. Women, native Americans and negroes, many of whom were still slaves, were all excluded from the dream of freedom, all pushed to the side of society: even in the Brave New World which Fowles presents as more attractive and vigorous than England, women were excluded. Sarah Woodruff can be viewed as a feminist heroine because though pushed to the side of society, she is not pushed to the side of her own life. She chooses the role of outcast because in Existentialist terms making a choice, even a difficult one which may be bewildering or incomprehensible to others, is to give your life a direction and to take control for yourself. Sarah plans and executes her seduction of Charles and manages happily to live with its consequences. By the end of the novel she is, if not quite independent (all freedoms are relative), useful, creative and valued: in short a great deal freer than she was in Lyme and is controlled by no man.

Sexuality

Fowles writes an interesting digression in Chapter 35 about Victorian sexuality. He begins with the disclosure that Mary was not a virgin and

---

Pause for *Thought*

When the novel's title is analysed in the light of feminist critique, we see that Fowles is being heavily ironic. Victorian notions of women 'belonging' to men may well lead the residents of Lyme to describe Sarah as 'The French Lieutenant's Woman' — or worse — but Sarah is not and never has been Varguennes's or anyone else's woman. She belongs to and is responsible for herself. Why do you think female freedom is so important to Fowles?

PHILIP ALLAN LITERATURE GUIDE FOR A-LEVEL

therefore understood perfectly well what was afoot between Charles and Sarah in the barn. Fowles's essay gives his thoughts on Victorian 'sublimation': the damming and diverting of the great canal of sex into other activities into which middle-class, educated Victorians poured themselves, at least in public. Fowles here utilises a Freudian analysis; however, he also describes differences in attitude between middle- and working-class Victorians, for which he adopts a Marxist perspective: working people, especially the rural poor, subscribed to the tradition of 'tasting before you buy' while middle-class commentators looked on aghast from the vantage point of bourgeois morality.

An account of Thomas Hardy's five-year love affair with his cousin Tryphena Sparks is also given in this chapter: the engagement was broken off not because Hardy had risen too far up the social ladder to be happy with a simple Dorset girl (Tryphena was 'exceptional': very intelligent and successful, so in many ways like Sarah Woodruff) but because she was Hardy's 'illegitimate half-sister's illegitimate daughter' (p. 274). Sexual conduct can have lasting consequences and our choices can have a lasting effect on our happiness. Sarah finds freedom through sexuality, although she ensnares Charles while attempting it; not quite an egalitarian *quid pro quo* but something Sarah feels she needs to do at the time. It would appear that Fowles wants to make his readers see Sarah's seduction of Charles as an example of the freedom she has given herself by creating the 'mask' of the French Lieutenant's Woman. The freedom she enjoys is both feminist and Existentialist. Fowles argues that we have to fulfil our natural sexual desires in a healthy way, free from concepts of duty and morality; as the case of Marie de Morell shows, this is difficult to achieve in rigid societies which place sanctions on all sexual conduct but especially on the sexual conduct of women. Madame Bovary could not make her sexual revolution end happily but Sarah Woodruff succeeds.

Victorian values

Chapter 39 includes a discourse on Victorian prostitution, an occupation which was condemned but which flourished none the less. In terms of the capitalist notion of market forces, prostitution would not exist unless there was a demand for it. In Marxist terms it is another form of exploitation. Once again Sarah manages to rise above the Victorian age by her decision to place herself to the side of conventional society and consequently enjoy a degree of sexual liberty not sullied by market forces or twisted into a grotesque shape by Christianity.

Pause for *Thought*

In a footnote in Chapter 28 Fowles tells his readers that there were more shocking revelations about the de La Roncière case, claiming that the events of the night of the alleged assault were 'obscene and absurd', citing René Floriot's *Les Erreurs Judiciaires* (p. 236). Why do you think Fowles does not tell us the ultimate truth but sends readers to a French book (still) not printed in English?

Context

Actually Miss Allen's lover and tormented by Marie's campaign of lies, de La Roncière got drunk and vowed revenge. Turning up at the house, he staggered into Marie's bedroom, lifted her nightgown and snipped off some of her pubic hair (a souvenir of the revenge), then fled. The young women then concocted their plan and informed Marie's parents. During the trial de La Roncière was too ashamed to say what he had done.

Depictions of Victorian Christianity feature prominently in the text. Fowles, an atheist, savagely satirises Mrs Poulteney's hideous version of Christianity on many occasions, but in Chapter 48 when Charles is praying in the church in Exeter we see a more contemplative view. 'Intelligent and sensitive' Victorians, so Fowles tells us, believed in charity as a means of being closer to God and felt more personally responsible than we do, living in an age where the welfare state makes charity fully organised and government-administered. It was much harder for Victorians to reject Christ the 'universal symbol of compassion' (p. 362) than it is for us. The implication is that we should not see all Victorian Christians merely as stupid bigots like Mrs Poulteney but that for the decent-minded, Christian charity was a vehicle for much-needed poor-relief. Charles 'in the dark Gothic Church' was 'not weeping for Sarah, but for his own inability to speak to God' (p. 362), thereby demonstrating that Charles's agnosticism is hardening, if not into atheism, then into a position that rejects all versions of organised religion as pointless. In this way, with Fowles using Charles as a sort of moral **Everyman**, the reader is shown how British society progressed from its drone-like devotion to 'gloomy' Christianity to its modern, healthier rejection of it. Once again Fowles is analysing society in terms of his own interests in Marxism and Existentialism, describing how Charles discovers he has to reject Christianity because it is enslaving him: organised Christianity is a death-cult in which Charles does not have to believe because it condemns its followers to 'a life in the grave' (p. 368).

Interestingly, Charles does not reject Jesus but sees his life as an example of a kind of rebellion, as an example of rejecting traditional moral values to become free. Once he has rejected Christianity and secularised Jesus, Charles sees the wonderful opportunities and potentials of 'another world: a new reality, a new causality, a new creation' (p. 368) which will not haunt him with ideas of guilt, sin, judgement and damnation. Fowles is clear that the rejection of Christian Victorian values is part of the path to freedom.

Everyman

an ordinary person, a typical representative of the human race

Taking it
Further ➤

Read *Tess of the D'Urbervilles* or *Jude the Obscure* to understand why Fowles so admired Hardy and to get a sense of the heavy use of coincidence and improbable plot twists in Victorian fiction.

Thomas Hardy's later novels

Fowles loved Hardy's work and in the novel he makes respectful, occasionally playful, use of *Tess of the d'Urbervilles* and *Jude the Obscure* as intertextual material.

Links between Hardy's and Fowles's work are many but here are some of the more obvious connections:

- Hardy uses epigraphs and footnotes in *Jude*, so Fowles does in *The French Lieutenant's Woman*.

- It is difficult not to see echoes of the real Tryphena Sparks (see pp. 273–74) in Sarah Woodruff, Sue Bridehead in *Jude*, and Tess.

- Sue, Tess and Sarah all get pregnant to men they are not married to and all are tormented by withering Victorian gossip.

- Jude and Sue and Sarah defy social norms and are outcasts from society as is Charles later in *The French Lieutenant's Woman*.

- Tess works temporarily at *Trantridge*; Fowles names his character Aunt *Tranter* in *The French Lieutenant's Woman*.

- Tess worked at *Talbothays*; Sarah worked for the *Talbots*.

- Sarah, like Tess, is the victim of her father's 'obsession with his own ancestry' (p. 54).

- Like Tess, Sarah's life turns on an undelivered letter.

- Fowles reverses the gender patterns: in *Tess of the d'Urbervilles* Alec seduces Tess, but in *The French Lieutenant's Woman* Sarah seduces Charles.

- Chapter 48 of *Tess of the d'Urbervilles* is structurally similar to Chapter 49 of *The French Lieutenant's Woman*, with Tess writing a letter to Angel Clare and Charles writing a letter to Sarah.

- Both Sarah and Tess get pregnant after one sexual encounter.

Task 5

Compare and contrast in terms of content and language the letters written by Tess to Angel in Chapter 48 (XLVIII) of *Tess of the D'Urbervilles* and by Charles to Sarah in Chapter 49 of *The French Lieutenant's Woman*. (There is also a Philip Allan Literature Guide (for A-Level) on *Tess of the D'Urbervilles*.)

Context

In *Tess of the D'Urbervilles*, Tess's father sends her to work for the nouveau-riche cad Alec D'Urberville, who rapes her. She has a child who dies and she later marries the naive Angel Clare. When Tess tells Angel of her past he abandons her. In desperation Tess goes back to Alec, but when Angel returns unexpectedly she murders Alec and runs away with Angel. She is captured and hanged.

Context

In *Jude the Obscure*, stonemason Jude Fawley is tricked into marrying vulgar Arabella Donn, who subsequently leaves him. Jude falls in love with his cousin Sue Bridehead, who marries Richard Phillotson. Sue leaves Phillotson to live with Jude, and they have two children. They also take in Arabella's son, but he murders their children before hanging himself. Believing this to be God's punishment, Sue goes back to Phillotson and Jude, now ill, dies alone.

Characters

Charles Smithson

Charles Smithson, the male protagonist, is 32, well-travelled and rich. An 'intelligent idler' with an interest in palaeontology, he is engaged to Ernestina Freeman; becomes attracted to the mysterious Sarah Woodruff and breaks his engagement after having sex with Sarah. The novel charts his life in Darwinian and Existentialist terms before and after his epoch-changing sexual encounter with the French Lieutenant's Woman.

Ernestina Freeman

Ernestina Freeman is a pretty, intelligent but spoilt only child, aged 22, who visits her Aunt Tranter in Lyme annually because of her parents' belief that the 'Channel breezes' are good for her health. Ernestina's room at Aunt Tranter's is 'gilt and fanciful' (p. 27), which reflects her nature. Her shallowness is satirised when she describes various priceless artefacts at Winsyatt as 'absurd…gloomy…moth-eaten and dull' (p. 192). She represents conventional Victorian womanhood.

Sarah Woodruff

Sarah Woodruff is the novel's 'wild' protagonist and central enigma. Aged around 25, she displays 'passion' and 'imagination' in orchestrating an affair with Charles. She is presented as both a modern and a Victorian woman. Fowles said he began to 'fall in love with her'. She is central in the novel's debates about social class, sexuality, freedom and identity.

Sam Farrow

Sam Farrow is Charles's cockney manservant who represents a 'social revolution Charles failed to recognise'. Sam is different from Dickens's Sam Weller from *The Pickwick Papers* who is 'happy' with his servant role whereas our Sam 'suffers' it. He represents the changing face of the Victorian working class.

Mary

Mary is Aunt Tranter's servant, happy now she has escaped Mrs Poulteney's clutches. Engaged to Sam, she is by 'far the prettiest' of the young women in the novel. She represents social change and beauty.

Aunt Tranter

Aunt Tranter, Ernestina's mother's sister, is a kind, honest woman who exerts a benign influence on everyone, the antithesis of Mrs Poulteney.

PHILIP ALLAN LITERATURE GUIDE **FOR A-LEVEL**

Mrs Poulteney

Mrs Poulteney is a bigoted Christian whose anti-life prejudice is demonstrated when she forbids Sarah to walk on the Cobb or Ware Commons, forcing her either not to walk anywhere or to defy her mistress. Her obsessions are 'Dirt' and 'Immorality': 'There would have been a place in the Gestapo' for her (p. 21).

Mrs Fairley

Mrs Fairley, Mrs Poulteney's sadistic housekeeper, spies on Sarah and the servants. She is a lackey, sharing her mistress's corrupt world-view.

Dr Grogan

Dr Grogan is intelligent, wise and liberal-minded, having tried to help Sarah escape the 'Bedlam' of Mrs Poulteney's house. He offers a scientific view of Sarah's behaviour: *'It [is] as if the woman had become addicted to melancholia as one becomes addicted to opium'* (pp. 156–57). Even Grogan is shocked at Charles's decision to abandon Ernestina.

Mr Freeman

Mr Freeman, Ernestina's father, owns a huge Oxford Street department store. He represents 'New Money' capitalism and offers a partnership in his business to the aristocratic Charles, who is appalled at the thought of 'going into trade'. Ironically, though he finds Darwin 'blasphemous', even Freeman sees the need to change with the times.

Other characters

- **Varguennes**, the 'French Lieutenant' of the title, does not appear in the novel. Sarah claims he seduced her and returned to France. She later discovered he was married. Sarah claims 'all he said was false' (p. 169) but since a lot of what Sarah says is false, he too is an enigma.

- **Mrs Bella Tomkins** does not appear directly in the novel but is described as a 'middle class adventuress' who marries Charles's Uncle Robert. She is presented as an agent of change in Darwinian and social terms.

- **Uncle Robert** is an old-fashioned aristocrat who disinherits Charles when he marries and fathers a child with Bella Tomkins.

- **Mr and Mrs Talbot** employ Sarah as a governess. It is at the Talbots' that she meets Varguennes.

Context

The Gestapo (abbreviation of **Ge**heime **St**aats**po**lizei) was the official secret police force of Nazi Germany and is regarded as one of the most evil organisations ever to have existed. It operated without judicial oversight and with complete carte blanche, and was responsible for the institution and administration of the Nazi concentration camps.

Form, structure and language

This section is designed to offer you information about the three strands of AO2. This Assessment Objective requires you to demonstrate detailed critical understanding in analysing the ways in which form, structure and language shape meanings in literary texts. To a certain extent these three terms should, as indicated elsewhere, be seen as fluid and interactive. Remember, however, that in the analysis of a novel such as *The French Lieutenant's Woman*, aspects of form and structure are at least as important as language. You should certainly not focus your study merely on lexical features of the text. Many features of form, structure and language in *The French Lieutenant's Woman* are further explored elsewhere in chapter summaries and in exemplar essays.

Form

Fowles writes a novel set between 1867 and 1869 that utilises many features of a traditional Victorian novel but also makes use of many Postmodern structures. An omniscient third person narrative common in Victorian literature is used, but Fowles uses the Postmodern technique of inserting himself into the narrative, either as an informative or friendly voice in the reader's ear or as a character who rides around with other characters on trains or jumps out of cabs to play tricks with Time.

> Fowles uses the Postmodern technique of inserting himself into the narrative

Early Victorian novels tended to present idealised versions of lives lived under adversity in which a certain doggedness of nature, perseverance, hard work, sexual and moral rectitude and good intentions bring reward to the central characters. Virtue is usually rewarded and villains and miscreants appropriately punished. Christianity is seen to work. Though perhaps with a morality not quite as simple as the model just outlined, Charlotte Brontë's *Jane Eyre* (1847) can still be read in the context of the fairly typical early Victorian novel. Yet as the age progressed more complex social and moral concerns began to emerge. Though writers still tended to view themselves as moral teachers (Fowles in 1964 claimed he was more teacher than novelist) the subject matter began to take on a darker tone. We have already seen what happened in France with the publication of *Madame Bovary*. In England Hardy was to suffer similar, though milder, criticism with the publication of *Tess of the d'Urbervilles* in 1891 and when *Jude the Obscure* was printed in 1895 the Bishop of Wakefield burned it in public, an act of Christian intolerance so perverse Mrs Poulteney would have approved. When Dickens published *The Pickwick Papers* in 1837 (featuring Sam Weller) the tone was comic, the mood light. When he came to write his tenth novel *Hard Times* in 1853 the tone was satirical and altogether more barbed as he railed against the inequalities and cruelties of the England he saw around him. Some novelists saw themselves as preachers of a sort and Fowles has great fun with this idea in Chapter 55 when he introduces himself into the story as 'a successful lay-preacher' with a Dickensian 'prophet-beard'.

Many Victorian novels were serialised and because of this they were often long; Fowles duly writes a novel of 445 pages. Victorian novels tended to be as close as possible to the real social conditions of their age, so after completing his first drafts of *The French Lieutenant's Woman* Fowles went over it line by line. He not only lengthened the sentences from his 1960s English into something longer and Victorianly Latinate, but repeatedly checked his facts to ensure that every important detail — from the time dundrearies stopped being fashionable to the dyes used in Victorian cloth-manufacturing — recreates the Victorian era with unmistakable veracity.

However, it is perhaps with his manipulation of traditional form that Fowles is most evidently subversive. Victorians loved cliff-hanger chapter endings largely as a consequence of the popularity of the serial novel, so Fowles gives us chapter endings which leave us in a state of suspense. Fowles concludes Chapter 29, for instance, with Charles peering fearfully over a partition in Carslake Barn. What will happen next? He makes us wait until Chapter 31 to tell us, inserting a chapter on how Sarah was dismissed by Mrs Poulteney in between. Who has discovered Charles and Sarah in the barn at the end of Chapter 31? We don't find out until Chapter 33. Rearranging the linear structure of the narrative is one of the aspects of Postmodernism that Fowles clearly likes.

Postmodernism

Postmodernism is notoriously hard to pin down but generally accepted features and how Fowles uses them are presented here.

Irony and playfulness

Irony and playfulness feature in the text, with Fowles making frequent asides, especially in relation to Charles's 'fossil' status and his various

Taking it Further

Jane Eyre recounts the heroine's life from orphan and abused child, to governess, to wife of her wealthy employer. The novel can be viewed either as a feminist critique of Victorian society, or as a wish-fulfilment fantasy in which a penniless girl joins the bourgeoisie by marriage. Dip in to *Jane Eyre*; how do you respond to it?

There are two opposing views of intertextuality: the first finds it an amusing means of allowing the reader to see that what we are reading is a construct operating within a range of other constructs; the other is that it is little more than a set of 'in-jokes' that distances the reader from the business of understanding character, ideas and plot. How do you react to the intertextuality in the novel?

Taking it **Further**

Read, or if at all possible see, a production of *Top Girls* and compare and contrast Churchill's use of historiographic metafiction with that used by Fowles.

non-linear narrative

a narrative where the storyline is presented out of chronological order

judgements on Victorian behaviour. His references to himself as a butler, a lay preacher, a dandified impresario who has 'gone in for grand opera' (p. 465) are playfully tongue-in-cheek. Most critics still miss the humour in *The French Lieutenant's Woman*.

Intertextuality

This is a term coined by Bulgarian/French academic Julia Kristeva in 1966 and means references or links to other texts, either by discussions of other work, or the adoption of a particular style. Fowles does both: he refers to many novels; he makes references to history, psychology, and science texts; inserts chunks of other people's essays and poetry; refers to art frequently and while doing so maintains a highly believable Victorian voice when it suits his purposes, which he is able to cast aside when he is being playful.

Metafiction

Metafiction means writing about writing ('foregrounding the apparatus'), making the artificiality of art apparent to the reader. It can be argued that it is not a specifically Postmodern device at all, for as early as 1759, Laurence Sterne's *The Life and Opinions of Tristram Shandy, Gentleman* was a novel about writing a novel. However, metafiction became much more popular in the twentieth century than it had been in the eighteenth. Metafiction must dispense with the 'willing suspension of disbelief' and is frequently employed to undermine the godlike authority of the author, for emotional distance, or to comment on the act of storytelling. Fowles clearly lets us know we are in a metafiction in Chapter 13 and reminds us of it throughout.

An offshoot of metafiction is historiographic metafiction, which is when writers fictionalise actual historical events or figures: Caryl Churchill's 1982 play *Top Girls* features a scene in which various female characters from history and fiction (Pope Joan, Dull Gret, Isabella Bird and Lady Nijo) meet Marlene, the play's central fictional character, at a dinner party. Fowles's work is obviously historical but in among his fictional characters he scatters Rossetti and Ruskin, though Rossetti only speaks ten words in the novel (all in Chapter 60) and Ruskin speaks not at all.

Temporal distortion

This is a common technique in modernist fiction, also popular in Postmodern fiction, where fragmentation and **non-linear narratives** demonstrate that kaleidoscopic meanings are possible. Time may overlap, repeat, or divide into multiple possibilities. The most well-known version of temporal distortion in modern popular culture is Harold Ramis's and Danny Rubin's 1993 film *Groundhog Day*, which shows a cynical weatherman having to live the same day over and over again. After many suicide attempts and forays into hedonism he chooses to emerge as a civilised and thoughtful human being. The film's links to Existentialism, though done with a light touch, are clear. In 2006 the film was added to the US National Film Registry as 'culturally, historically or aesthetically significant'. In Chapters 60 and 61 of *The French Lieutenant's Woman*, Fowles shows two possible versions of events that occupy the same time frame.

Taking it Further

Compare the 1993 comedy film *Groundhog Day*, starring Bill Murray, with the novel *The French Lieutenant's Woman*. What do these very different texts have to tell us about freedom?

Structure

The novel is divided into 61 chapters, each with at least one epigraph through which the novelist introduces the chapter's themes and ideas. These epigraphs are either genuinely Victorian (from 1837 to 1901), or modern texts about Victorianism, or are very occasionally from the 1960s (Chapter 20's epigraph is from William Manchester's *The Death of President Kennedy* and Chapter 61's is from Martin Gardner's *The Ambidextrous Universe*). In its consecutive chapter arrangement (1–61) the novel has a recognisable Victorian structure.

Significantly — and to keep up its Postmodern credentials — the novel presents the reader with *three* endings: the amusing, throwaway 'conventional' Victorian ending in Chapter 44, which is deliberately badly plotted and written as though the novelist had grown bored with the entire project (more Postmodern fun), and two 'final' chapters which are apparently offered as interchangeable.

Language

In a 1995 interview Fowles said: 'I adore language, and especially English with its incomparable richness. I think of that richness less as a doomed attempt to impose order on chaos than as an attempt to magnify reality. I have no time for the…belief that you must avoid all rare words and communicate by lowest common denominators alone. As well say you must use inferior tools.' The language of the novel, therefore, like the scholarship that adorns it, is rich and self-consciously ornate, just like a

Task 6

Look up 'exophthalmic' in a good dictionary. Why do you think Fowles uses this word in this context in Chapter 16? What does the adjective tell us:

a) about Sarah?

b) about what Fowles wants his readers to think about Sarah?

Task 7

Use a French dictionary to find out the meaning of *rondelet*. Why, when there is a dictionary definition available, do you think that Fowles claims it is a word 'for which we have no equivalent in English' (p. 75)? Are there any words in English that you may consider to be untranslatable in the sense that Fowles means?

bonafide Victorian novel should be. Fowles uses words that will send most readers scurrying for their dictionaries: in Chapter 54 when Charles goes back to his carriage he sinks into a state of 'aboulia' (a lack of will or motivation, usually manifested as an inability to make decisions or to set goals). In Chapter 16 he describes Sarah's eyes as 'exophthalmic'.

Sarah's eyes are very important: time and again Fowles describes them in such terms as 'fine', 'dark', 'abnormally large, as if able to see more and suffer more', 'intense', 'wide', 'sombre', 'sad' and 'direct'. Sarah's eyes haunt Charles for the whole novel and the adjectives that he uses to delineate their rare quality help create an overall image of her 'remarkable' nature. In Chapter 16 Charles is once again struck by the power of her eyes which 'could not conceal intelligence, an independence of spirit…a determination to be what she was' (p. 119). He also notices her eyes' 'suppressed intensity' and is reminded of 'foreign women… and foreign beds' (p. 120).

There are many fascinating opportunities to analyse Fowles's use of language in the novel and the following pages offer only a brief taste of Fowles at work.

In Chapter 11, Fowles's description on p. 75 of Mary's figure as '*rondelet*' (a French adjective) is interesting: he believes there are certain words (and by extension ideas) that will not translate directly from one language into another. This is the observation of a Francophile no doubt, but an important consideration for the reader is that in this novel there are certain ideas that the narrator claims lie beyond reason and rationality, beyond culture and convention. The enigma that is Sarah comes to mind.

Clothes take on an important symbolic function in the novel: Ernestina, while dressed in the very height of expensive, colourful fashion, still remains a silly, selfish child; Sarah's clothes are frequently described as black and masculine-looking and yet in Charles's mind do not reduce her femininity; Sam's dreams of a haberdashery shop reflect his interest in fashion not as mere adornment but as something real and practical. There are three stages to the colour symbolism of Sarah's clothes. In the early to middle part of the novel she wears black and indigo habitually. At Endicott's she wears a combination of white nightgown, red blanket and green shawl. In Chapters 60 and 61 she wears 'brilliant' colours of rich dark blue, crimson, pink and white stripes, white lace and red ribbon. The effect is 'electric and bohemian'. Her transformation is complete by this stage of Chapter 60, when she has 'winged from the black pupa' (p. 446).

Fowles makes much use of sexual language in Chapter 21 to heighten the sense of arousal Charles feels in Sarah's company: 'exposed', 'naked', 'penetration', 'nakedness', 'intimacy', 'frustration', 'lovers', 'erotic', 'kissed', 'thrown off her clothes', 'gently curving lips', 'stiffen', 'plunge', 'passionate', 'raised her skirts', 'lancing' are all suggestive of repressed but intense desire and are all predictors of what will happen later in Chapters 31 and 46.

In a novel of so many interesting chapters, Chapter 60 is in many ways the most interesting of all. A key idea in the chapter is how difficult it is for humans to understand each other: '**Language is like shot silk; so much depends on the angle at which it is held**' (p. 460). Fowles suggests that what is said is never as important as what is understood by what is said. Intended and received meanings are often at variance.

During their painful conversation Charles struggles to comprehend Sarah. The novelist even says they are speaking 'two languages' (p. 451) his is formal, hollow, foolishly constrained and artificial and hers is natural and direct. The consequence of this is that when she says something, he believes she has said something quite different.

We can break this conversation down into twelve key statements of Sarah's and twelve assumptions of Charles's (given in square brackets after each statement below) about what has just been said:

1 'I did not think ever to see you again' (p. 450). [She is someone's mistress, probably Rossetti's, despite her earlier denial.]

2 'I have forbidden myself to regret the impossible' (p. 450). [She thinks it is impossible that we can ever be lovers.]

3 'I *have* found new affections' (p. 450). [She *has* taken a lover.]

4 'I had thrown myself at you, forced myself upon you' (p. 451). [I have been the victim of a plot.]

5 'A madness was in me at that time' (p. 451). [She is making excuses for her past behaviour.]

6 'The natural had been adulterated by the artificial, the pure by the impure' (p. 451). [Sarah is intellectualising her bad behaviour to pass it off as an inferior work of art.]

7 'There is another.' [I *knew* it! She is somebody's mistress.]

8 'I do not wish to marry' (p. 453). [She does not wish to marry *me* but she is quite happy being this other man's mistress.]

9 'Mr Smithson, I am happy, I am at last arrived…where I belong' (p. 453). [She is being formal again just like in Exeter. She is happy here and she wants me to leave.]

10 'You do not understand…I am not to be understood' (p. 454). [She thinks I am not as intelligent and artistic as she is…and she is doing that enigmatic, artistic female act again.]

11 'I…saw one of the notices you had had put in…I knew then… that you had not married Miss Freeman' (p. 455). [She lied about not knowing I have been looking for her. She is malicious, manipulative, scheming and cruel: an accomplished actress.]

12 'There is a lady in this house who knows me…She will explain…my real nature far better than I can myself' (p. 457). [Another woman! Who understands her real nature? With her proven hatred of man?… This strange bohemian crowd! Christina Rossetti, 'the sobbing abbess', the hysterical spinster — she lives in this house! I have heard the rumours! What new enormity?…Sarah is a lesbian!]

Task 8

Write an essay with the title 'Analyse Charles's relationship with Sarah throughout the novel in the light of the statement 'Language is like shot silk; so much depends on the angle at which it is held' (p. 460).

Only when Lalage is placed on the carpet does Charles realise the truth and work out that it was not Sarah's odd individualism or sexual nature that was the driving force in her life, but her new condition of motherhood. What we infer is not always what was meant to be conveyed. We make our own meaning. This is an idea integral to Postmodern thought. In this ending of the novel Sarah and Charles look at each other intently. 'Such looks we have all once or twice in our lives received and shared; they are those in which worlds melt, pasts dissolve, moments when we know…that the rock of ages can never be anything else but love' (p. 462). So Fowles cleverly manages to give his readers a conventional happy ending for a Victorian novel which has been wrapped around an intriguing little discourse on how fraught and difficult it is to arrive at a coherent, shared understanding.

Contexts

Biographical context

John Fowles was born in Leigh-on-Sea, Essex, on 31 March 1926. His father was a well-to-do cigar importer and lawyer whose lifelong interest in philosophy inspired his son to think about the world of ideas. His mother, a Cornish ex-schoolteacher, fired his imagination about Celtic literature and myth.

Fowles was educated at Bedford School, then went to Edinburgh University, but was called up as a lieutenant in the Royal Marines (1945–46), which he roundly detested. However, the Second World War ended before he saw combat. His unhappy military service is described in his foreword to the 1974 edition of *The Hound of the Baskervilles*. After the war he attended New College, Oxford, where he read French. After leaving Oxford he taught English Literature at the University of Poitiers (France) and English on the Greek island of Spetsai where he worked at Anargyrios College, run on Eton-and-Harrow lines for Greece's future leaders. On Spetsai, Fowles met Elizabeth Christy (a married woman with a daughter, Anna). Three years later, on 2 April 1954, she and Fowles were married in England, where Fowles got a teaching job at St Godric's College, London. The marriage was to last thirty-seven years until Elizabeth's death from cancer in 1990 and Fowles frequently remarked that Elizabeth was behind 'every female character' he wrote about in one way or another.

While teaching, an occupation he followed until 1963, Fowles was also trying to write *The Magus* and a dozen novels all abandoned as being 'incomplete or too lengthy'. However, he managed to write *The Collector* in one intense month in 1960, but revised it until summer 1962 before submitting it to a publisher. It appeared in 1963 to instant success and he gave up teaching to become a full-time writer. *The Aristos* (Greek: 'the best'), a philosophical work, was published in 1964, followed one year later by *The Magus*, which was even more popular than *The Collector*.

In 1968 Fowles and his family settled in Lyme Regis, Dorset, where he lived in happy exile from the literary circles of London. Here he quietly wrote and followed his other hobbies, mainly focusing on local and

natural history and botany. He developed an interest in archaeology, and like Charles in the novel went fossil-hunting on the nearby cliffs. He became curator of Lyme Regis Museum in 1979, a position he held with some pride for ten years until a stroke made him too ill to continue to work. He recovered from most of the serious effects of the stroke and married his second wife Sarah in 1998. He died in 2005 after a long battle with a heart problem.

Of his upbringing in Leigh, Fowles commented that it was 'dominated by conformism—the pursuit of respectability…The rows of respectable little houses inhabited by respectable little people had an early depressive effect on me and I believe that they caused my intense and continuing dislike of mankind *en masse.*'

It has been said that Fowles's writing is too cold for readers to like but book sales alone attest to his popularity. Fowles was a self-confessed misanthropist: his early opposition to conformity and the forces of middle-class English Puritanism gave him a strong sense of individualism which made him interested in the exploration of ideas concerning freedom, a subject that emerges in many of his works. When remembering his time at boarding school (Bedford), which he started in 1939, he claimed that he became 'adept at wearing masks' to hide his true feelings: 'I suffer from it like every one of my type and background. I've played the game all my life.' This '**masque**' theme (part repression, part secrecy, part game-playing, part acting) emerges in much of his fiction as Fowles's characters adopt roles, play parts and frequently simply lie: sometimes their internal development is thwarted by such tactics, at other times characters enjoy a measure of success and fulfilment. Sarah Woodruff can be seen as an adept mask-wearer.

masque a form of dramatic entertainment popular with the aristocracy in sixteenth and seventeenth century England, which consisted of dancing and acting by lavishly costumed masked performers

By the end of his time at Bedford School, Fowles was captain of the cricket First Eleven and Head Boy. There is much of the early Fowles in Charles Smithson: a man driven by ideas about freedom but conforming to a sense of duty before a life-changing rebellion. Fowles admitted he did not like the power and status of being Head Boy: 'By the age of 18, I had had dominion over 600 boys, and learned all about power, hierarchy and the manipulation of law. Ever since I have had a violent hatred of leaders, organisers, bosses — of anyone who thinks it good to get or have arbitrary power over other people.' His parents moved to Devon in 1940 to escape the danger of air-raids, which he describes factually in his essay *The Tree* (1979). He would visit his parents during holidays and the simple patterns of village life and the rural idyll affected Fowles forever. The natural beauty caught his imagination to such an extent that he constantly maintained that nature was not only his primary interest but also 'the key to my fiction' (*The Tree*). Sarah Woodruff is frequently portrayed as an elemental creature in the early part of the novel, finding comfort within natural environments.

Oxford, like Devon, fired Fowles's imagination. He referred to his time at Oxford as 'three years of heaven in an intellectual sense', and it was during this time that he learned more about Celtic romances and discovered the work of the French Existentialists. His experience of the mystery and majesty of Spetsai was as powerful an influence on him as Devon or Oxford had been. Not only did he write poetry, which appeared later in his collection *Poems*, but Spetsai also provided the inspiration for *The Magus*, a work that would obsess the writer for a quarter of a century. Leaving Greece was a painful experience, but one that Fowles saw as having been necessary to his artistic growth. 'I had not then realised that loss is essential for the novelist, immensely fertile for his books, however painful to his private being.' Loss is a key feature in Fowles's work and could be said to dominate *The French Lieutenant's Woman* almost as much as freedom.

The Collector is the story of Frederick Clegg, a poorly educated, deeply unattractive bank clerk (one of the masses) and butterfly-collector, who becomes obsessed with beautiful young art student, Miranda Grey (one of the few). Clegg wins a fortune on the football pools, enabling him to carry out his plan of kidnap and imprisonment. The narrative shifts, with the first part of the book told from Clegg's point of view and the second recounting the imprisoned Miranda's perspective. The characters of Miranda and Clegg, set in opposition, embody the conflict that Fowles, via Heraclitus in Ancient Greece, finds central to mankind: the few versus the many; the artistic versus the conventional; the *aristoi* versus *hoi polloi*; the individual versus the herd. As Fowles noted, 'My purpose in *The Collector* was to analyse, through a parable, some of the results of this confrontation'. Miranda, according to Fowles, 'is an Existential heroine although she doesn't know it. She's groping for her own authenticity...*The Collector* is to show that our world is sick,' 'The slow degrees' by which Clegg destroys Miranda, wrote Alan Pryce-Jones in *The New York Times Book Review*, 'make one of the most agonising chapters in the whole literary history of obsession.'

Fowles's next published work, *The Magus* (1965) was 'in every way except that of mere publishing date...a first novel'. Nicholas Urfe, a callow English schoolmaster, meets magus Maurice Conchis (part Prospero in *The Tempest*, part Aleister Crowley from real life), the master of an island estate which in homage to Fowles's much-loved *Le Grand Meaulnes* is called a 'domaine'. Through a series of sometimes terrifying,

---

Context

It could be argued that Sarah is on a series of journeys, actual and metaphorical, within the novel: she moves from the wild exteriors of the Cobb and the Undercliff (Lyme Regis) to the bohemian interiors of Rossetti's house (London), and transforms her appearance from a black-clad figure to a colourful and vibrant New Woman. Walking and travelling feature prominently in the novel, perhaps as symbols of the various emotional journeys the characters make.

sometimes beautiful 'godgames', Conchis breaks down and destroys Nicholas's perception of reality, a 'necessary step' towards the 'true understanding' of his being in the world. *The Magus* has an Existentialist heart.

Among the seven novels that Fowles wrote, *The Magus* has generated the most fanatical interest and is still a cult novel, being both a complex experiment in quest literature and an essay on the nature of reality which bears comparison to Homer's *Odyssey*. Fowles both entertains and philosophises in *The Magus* and makes his readers question ideas concerning freedom, 'hazard' and the uncertainties presented by existence. Fowles compared it to a detective story because of the way it teases its readers: 'You mislead them ideally to lead them into a greater truth…it's a trap which I hope will hook the reader.' Fowles issued a revised edition in 1977 in which he had rewritten numerous scenes in an attempt to 'purify' the work he called an 'endlessly tortured and recast cripple' which had, nonetheless, 'aroused more interest than anything else I have written'. Fowles wrote the screenplay for the film version of *The Magus* and even had a little cameo role in it, but considered it a disaster and vowed never to write another script from his own work. Woody Allen is reported to have said, when asked whether he would live his life differently if given the chance, that he would do everything the same — except watch *The Magus*.

The genesis of *The French Lieutenant's Woman* is revealing: Fowles saw a 'vision' one morning in 1966 in that 'hypnagogic state between waking and sleeping' of an enigmatic, solitary woman, standing on the Cobb at Lyme Regis, staring off into the distant sea, a woman who 'clearly belonged to the past'. In an article for *Harper's Magazine*, he wrote, 'The woman obstinately refused to stare out of the window of an airport lounge; it had to be this ancient quay.' The image of the woman haunted him. He notes that she had 'no face, no particular degree of sexuality. But she was Victorian; and since I always saw her in the same static long shot, with her back turned, she represented a reproach on the Victorian Age. An outcast. I didn't know her crime, but I wished to protect her. That is, I began to fall in love with her. Or with her stance. I didn't know which.' The vision recurred, became an obsession, and led eventually to *The French Lieutenant's Woman*.

After writing the first draft in about nine months, he spent the next two years revising, working line-by-line to create the illusion of Victorian prose and dialogue by lengthening sentences, deleting contractions and employing digressions. The novelist claimed that the key idea in the text was freedom: 'The whole human condition is slavery, and self-liberation is that little flash in the darkness for the individual.' *The French Lieutenant's Woman* was Fowles's major critical and financial success and earned him both the Silver Pen and the W. H. Smith Literary Awards in 1970 when it was the second most popular novel in the United States, only being beaten by Erich Segal's *Love Story*. It was made into an acclaimed film of the same name in 1981 with a screenplay by Harold Pinter. Fowles enjoyed the film, which was nominated for five Academy awards and which won three BAFTAs.

TopFoto

John Fowles in 1982. On one of the occasions on which he inserts himself into the novel he appears as a 'bearded stranger' (Chapter 55); and the farmer at the Dairy, which was based on Fowles's home at the time, Underhill Farm, is described as 'a vast-bearded man with a distinctly saturnine cast to his face: a Jeremiah'.

Throughout his career, Fowles committed himself to a scholarly exploration of the place of the artist in society and sought the personal isolation and exile that he felt essential to such a search. In this regard he resembles Nicholas in *The Magus* and Charles at the end of *The French Lieutenant's Woman*, who have discovered themselves through a painful quest. A very learned man, Fowles deserves his high reputation as an innovator in the evolution of the modern novel. He was immersed in and profoundly excited by science, yet believed that what humankind needed was 'the existence of mysteries. Not their solutions.' Fowles could be curmudgeonly but was also a man of charm, grace and kindness. Much as it frustrated some of his readers, Fowles always believed he had done the right thing by leaving the endings of his most celebrated novels open-ended. His nature as a man and as a novelist is perhaps best revealed by the following story.

Pause for *Thought*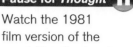

Watch the 1981 film version of the novel. Excellent and clever though the film undoubtedly is, Harold Pinter left out various aspects of the original novel and inserted new features not found in Fowles. What do you think is lost and gained by these changes?

He told an interviewer that he had received 'a sweet letter' from a terminal cancer patient in New York who wanted very much to believe that Nicholas, in *The Magus*, was reunited with Alison at the end of the book. 'Yes, of course they were,' Fowles replied, rewarding the correspondent. By chance, he had received a letter the same day from an irate reader taking issue with the ending of *The Magus*. 'Why can't you say what you mean, and for God's sake, what happened in the end?' the reader asked. Fowles said he found the letter 'horrid' but 'had the last laugh', supplying an alternative ending to punish the correspondent: 'They never saw each other again.'

Historical, social and cultural contexts

Freud

Sigmund Freud (1856–1939) was an Austrian neurologist now best known for his theories of the subconscious mind, the notion of repression and for creating the clinical practice of psychoanalytical 'talk therapy' between doctor and patient. Freud is also renowned for his redefinition of sexual desire as the primary motivational energy of human life. This notion of the importance of sexual desire, especially repressed sexual desire, has made his hypotheses very popular with some writers and literary critics, especially when such ideas were comparatively new between the 1920s and 1950s.

In terms of *The French Lieutenant's Woman* it is useful to have a brief overview of Freud's notions of the id, the ego and the super-ego. According to Freud's ideas, the id is the set of uncoordinated instinctual urges humans feel; the ego is the organised, realistic part of the mind; and the super-ego plays the critical and moralising role. Freud's structural model of the psyche (Greek: 'soul, mind, breath, life', which the Greeks believed were all collectively responsible for human behaviour but which Freud reduced to the concept of the mind alone) was first outlined in *Beyond the Pleasure Principle* (1920) and was formalised and elaborated upon three years later in his *The Ego and the Id*.

The id

The id comprises the random and uncoordinated part of the personality structure which contains the basic drives, acting according to the 'pleasure principle', seeking to avoid pain. Freud described it as 'a cauldron full of seething excitations…filled with energy reaching from the instincts, but it has no organisation, produces no collective will, but only a striving to bring about the satisfaction of the instinctual needs.' Freud believed that the mind of a newborn child is completely 'id-ridden', in the sense that it is a mass of instinctive drives and impulses, and needs immediate satisfaction.

The id, amoral and selfish, is responsible for our basic drives and urges such as for food and sex. Freud divided the id's 'drives and instincts' into two categories: life and death instincts. Life instincts (*Eros*, Greek: intimate sexual love) are those that are crucial to pleasurable survival, such as eating and sexual intercourse. The Death instinct (*Thanatos* in Greek mythology was the god of non-violent death, whose touch was gentle, like that of his twin brother Hypnos) is our subconscious wish to die, as *Thanatos* puts an end to the everyday struggles for happiness and survival. Freud believed he saw the death instinct in our desire for peace and in our attempts to escape reality through fiction, media and drugs. The poet John Keats (1795–1821) confessed himself to be 'half in love with easeful Death' (*Ode to a Nightingale*), and many other writers have expressed a similar sentiment, so it is apparent that Freud has found something in the idea of *Thanatos* that resonates.

> **Context**
>
> The Greek poet Hesiod writes that Thanatos and Hypnos are the sons of Nyx (Night) and Erebos (Darkness). Homer also mentions them in the *Iliad*. Freud understood the symbolic nature of Greek mythology — in particular how the Greeks ascribed human characteristics to their gods — and found the symbolism useful.

The ego

The ego acts according to what Freud called 'the reality principle', seeking to please the id's drive in realistic ways that will benefit the organism in the long term rather than bringing catastrophe or tragedy. The ego helps us to organise our thoughts to make sense of them, fitting them to the world around us. 'The ego is that part of the id which has been modified by the direct influence of the external world…The ego represents what may be called reason and common sense, in contrast to the id, which contains the passions…Its task is to find a balance between primitive drives and reality…Its main concern is with the individual's safety and it allows some of the id's desires to be expressed.' To Freud, then, the ego is the part of the mind that contains the consciousness. Originally, Freud used the word *ego* to mean a sense of self, but later revised it to mean a set of psychic control functions including judgement, tolerance, planning, synthesis of information, intellectual reasoning and memory.

The super-ego

The super-ego controls our sense of right and wrong and 'aims for perfection'. It can be thought of as a type of conscience that punishes misbehaviour with feelings of guilt. For example the feelings of self-loathing and fear when having extra-marital affairs can be claimed as the work of the super-ego, which operates in contradiction to the id. The super-ego helps us fit into society by getting us to act in socially acceptable ways.

Freud and *The French Lieutenant's Woman*

Though the characters in *The French Lieutenant's Woman* do not consider such concepts themselves, not having access to the vocabulary which will enable them to rationalise their lives in Freudian terms, Fowles wishes his readers to consider a psychological analysis of character.

Actions in the novel can be interpreted in a Freudian way. In Chapter 5, when Ernestina has a 'wicked' sexual thought, her response of 'I must not' (p. 30) is the super-ego retaliation of her subconscious mind to drive away the 'howling wolf' of the id. Conversely, in Chapter 46 when Sarah's id tells her she desires Charles sexually — earlier seductive ploys having failed — she feigns a strained ankle, wears her most feminine clothes, removes her underwear and waits for him to arrive.

Fowles's implication is that unless human beings learn to accommodate the force of the id we are doomed to be repressed. As long as the super-ego is allowed to override natural urges with unnatural concepts such as duty and inauthentic morality, we will remain trapped. Sarah liberates herself because her ego rationalises her desire for Charles and allows her to achieve that desire; though Sarah may not be consciously aware of it, the purchase of the bandage and the green shawl certainly shows an ordering of her thoughts consistent with the function of the ego which allows her to fulfil her id-driven desires.

We may look at much of Charles's behaviour in a Freudian light. Though id-fulfilment was easier for Victorian men than Victorian women, Fowles makes it clear as early as Chapter 3 that Charles's natural reaction to sexual behaviour is guilt. When in his second year at Cambridge he had woken up beside a naked cockney girl, he had rushed from her arms into those of the Church, announcing to his father that he intended to take Holy Orders. His hedonistic father, horrified at the prospect of his son frittering his life away on religion, dispatched him to six months in

Paris, the 'City of Sin' whence Charles returned in 1856 with his tarnished virginity 'blackened out of recognition' (p. 15). In the course of his other travels he has had sexual relations with foreign women of a lower social class and has learned to come to terms with his own sexual behaviour. In Freudian terms his ego has rationalised his id-based desires and enabled him to justify his behaviour as adding to his experience, making him a man of the world, increasing his store of urbane sophistication. Yet with Charles the super-ego is highly prominent: he searches for perfection and is never quite happy with himself suffering from feelings of 'obscure defeat'. When Fowles says 'You will see that Charles set his sights high' (p. 17), he is hinting that as well as being unrealistic in the conscious world, Charles is a man whose super-ego will demand that Charles be 'over-fastidious' in his subconscious mind. He experiences guilt following every sexual encounter he has: the kiss in the barn with Sarah in Chapter 31, the night with Sarah the prostitute in Chapter 40 and especially the sexual intercourse with Sarah in Chapter 46; these all demonstrate that despite Charles's surface self-assurance and sang-froid his super-ego still dominates and imprisons him.

Taking it **Further** ➤

Read Keats's 'Ode to a Nightingale' in the light of the Freudian ideas outlined in this section and see how useful and interesting it is to adopt a Freudian analytical approach to literary enquiry.

Darwin and the theory of evolution

Charles Darwin (1809–82) was an English naturalist famous for his proposition of the world-changing theory of evolution. In 1828 at Cambridge University where Darwin had gone with a view to enter the Anglican Church, after having previously studied medicine at Edinburgh, he met the eminent botanist John Stevens Henslow. It was Henslow who encouraged Darwin's interest in zoology and geology and who recommended him as a naturalist to *HMS Beagle*, then about to undertake detailed hydrographic surveys in South American waters.

During the expedition (1831–36), which Darwin wrote about in the travelogue now published as *The Voyage of the Beagle*, he amassed a huge knowledge of the fauna, flora and geology of lands unknown in scientific terms to European academics. At 1832 in Punta Alta he made a major fossil find, about which he wrote excitedly to Henslow: he had discovered the outer shell of the extinct *glyptodont*, a massive armadillo. As the journey continued he collected and made detailed observations of plants and animals, with results that continued to shake his Linnaean belief that species were fixed. The Galapagos Islands fascinated him: 'Considering the small size of these islands, we feel the more astonished at the number of their aboriginal beings and at their confined range…within a period geologically recent the unbroken

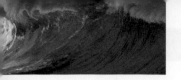

ocean was here spread out. Hence, both in space and time, we seem to be brought somewhat near to that great fact — that mystery of mysteries — the first appearance of new beings on this earth.' While aboard the *Beagle* his ideas developed and he continued to investigate and test his hypotheses when he returned to England.

As early as 1842 Darwin had arrived at his theory of evolution and by 1844 had written a 230-page essay which he kept among his private papers, fearing the storm of protest that would inevitably ensue if he made his knowledge public. This work demonstrated that variation exists among individuals of a species and that scarcity of resources in a burgeoning population leads to competition between individuals of the same species because all use the same resources. Such competition would lead to the death of some individuals, while others would survive. From this reasoning Darwin concluded that individuals having advantageous variations are more likely to survive and reproduce than those without advantageous variations. Darwin coined the term *natural selection* to describe the process by which organisms with favourable variations survive and reproduce at a higher rate. When species adapt, evolution by natural selection occurs and, in turn, natural selection leads ultimately to the formation of new species.

Science could now prove that the Creation story in the Bible was false, and Darwin, who fully understood the momentous implications of his theory, decided not to publish. However, in 1858 Albert Russell Wallace unexpectedly sent Darwin a paper he had written about the life forms on the Malay Archipelago which coincided with Darwin's opinions about natural selection. Darwin's scientific friends, led by Sir Charles Lyell and Joseph Hooker, persuaded him to publish a paper which was read alongside Wallace's before the Linnaean Society on 1 July 1858, with neither Wallace nor Darwin being present at the historic occasion. The meeting passed off barely noticed beyond the small academic crowd that had gathered.

Darwin spent the next year organising his huge array of notes and subsequently in November 1859 published *The Origin of Species by Means of Natural Selection*. The anti-Genesis implication of the work was understood immediately and in consequence Darwin was both violently attacked and energetically defended throughout Europe and America. In *The French Lieutenant's Woman* Charles and Grogan are passionately committed Darwinists and celebrate the 'great man's… great new truths' over cigars and grog, thereby proving their progressive credentials to the reader, whereas Mr Freeman says 'You will never get me to agree that we are all descended from monkeys. I find that idea blasphemous' (p. 290), demonstrating his conservative Christianity.

Darwin added to his groundbreaking, epoch-making masterpiece with various supplements throughout the rest of his life, the most controversial of which was *The Descent of Man and Selection in Relation to Sex* (1871), which argued that the human race had evolved from a 'hairy quadruped' related to the progenitors of the orang-utan, chimpanzee and gorilla. 'Well, I'll be a monkey's uncle!' is a humorous phrase from around this time. The popular satirical magazine *Punch* joined in the fun.

MAN·IS·BVT·A·WORM·

A Punch cartoon of 1882 satirising Darwin's theories

Darwin and *The French Lieutenant's Woman*

Charles represents the Darwinian strand in the novel: as he struggles to adapt to his changing environment he is threatened with extinction. Fowles refers to him as 'a fossil' on many occasions. In Chapter 48 Charles begins to discover the advantages of adapting to his new environment, but he still shows some of the vestigial traces of his old form throughout Chapters 49 to 58. He only truly begins to evolve in the USA (the New World) in Chapter 59.

> Fowles refers to Charles as 'a fossil' on many occasions

In the 'ending' of Chapter 60 Charles does not quite evolve fully because, leaving Victorian literary ideas about happy endings to one side, to accept a relationship with Sarah and Lalage will be to accept another form of duty which will compromise his new-found freedom. Charles would be choosing a different method of extinction. The ending of Chapter 61 is far more satisfactory in Darwinian terms because Charles accepts that to compromise by giving away the 'atom of faith in himself' he has just discovered in America is to allow himself to be manipulated towards his own extinction in an environment he has not selected. Scientists and individualists prefer the ending of Chapter 61; romantics and conformists prefer the ending of Chapter 60 both of which, in evolutionary terms, are examples of what may happen to a species.

Critical context

Marxism

Fowles was interested in the philosophies of Karl Marx (1818–1883), the German philosopher and revolutionary thinker perhaps most famous for his argument 'The history of all hitherto existing society is the history of class struggles' (*Communist Manifesto*, 1848). It is useful to have an overview of Marxist philosophy concerning social class, the categorisation of which derives from an individual's relationship to the *means of production*.

The proletariat

The proletariat consists of those individuals who sell their labour and who do not own the means of production. A factory owner will exploit his workers because the workers' labour generates a profit greater than the worker's wages. Sam is an interesting character as he represents the urban proletariat in many ways but since he is the servant of an aristocrat he has several features of the peasantry, while his dreams of owning his own small business are distinctly petit bourgeois.

The bourgeoisie

The bourgeoisie consists of those people who own the means of production and buy labour from the proletariat. The bourgeoisie — along with the landlords — are the seven per cent of the population that owns 84 per cent of the wealth. According to Marxist economic analysis this 7:84 ratio was accurate in Victorian times and is still a pretty accurate reflection of wealth distribution in today's Britain, though non-Marxist economic analysts disagree. Because the bourgeoisie owns the vast majority of a nation's capital wealth (money) this group is known as capitalists, and the complex, integrated system it invented and uses to run society for its own interests is known as capitalism.

The petite bourgeoisie consists of people who employ labourers in a minor way, run small businesses or act as peasant landlords. Marxism predicts that the continual reinvention and upgrading of the means of production will eventually destroy the petite bourgeoisie, degrading them from the middle class to the proletariat. In this way the current trend for major supermarket chains to put out of business small local shops can be viewed as the bourgeoisie destroying the petite bourgeoisie. Greed will eat itself.

The careful student will now notice the many links between Darwinism and Marxism. Mr Freeman and Ernestina are the novel's representatives of the bourgeoisie. It is significant that Sam's dreams of independence are thwarted and in classic Marxist style his petit bourgeois aspirations are swallowed up by the bourgeois machine of commerce. 'Freeman's for Choice' is a slogan we have to take ironically.

The lumpenproletariat

The lumpenproletariat are the criminals, beggars and other outcasts, who have no stake in the economy, and so sell their labour irregularly and fitfully to the highest bidder, or do not sell it at all. In more recent times the lumpenproletariat can be categorised as the 'underclass' who live on benefits. Think of the audience and participants in *The Jeremy Kyle Show*. State benefits were not an option in Victorian England. In Marxist analysis, these people tend to coagulate at the bottom of the social hierarchy where they form a lumbering lump.

Though able to function within her self-imposed exile from the norms of a restrictive society in Lyme, Sarah is threatened with the frightening prospect of becoming a prostitute should she go to a big city. Sarah the prostitute from Chapters 39 and 40 is a representative of the lumpenproletariat. Note that Marx and Fowles have sympathy with the lumpenproletariat that have been cast aside and categorised as useless by capitalism. In Marxism, raising the class consciousness of the lumpenproletariat via education and providing decent housing, welfare and jobs are the key ingredients of social justice.

The landlords

In Marxist terms, the landlords are aristocrats and landowners who retain considerable power. Charles's Uncle Robert is such a landlord and for a good portion of the novel Charles is the heir to Winsyatt. In Chapter 39 we meet other representatives of the landlord class in Charles's London Club in the form of the oafs Tom and Nat. When Charles's uncle marries Bella Tomkins and subsequently fathers a son, Charles is disinherited. Mr Freeman offers Charles the opportunity of becoming a member of the bourgeoisie but Charles is appalled at the prospect of 'going into trade' and eventually is effectively neither a representative of the bourgeoisie into which he has been invited nor of the landlord class into which he has been born. This apparent classlessness can be interpreted either as an advantage or as a disadvantage to Charles's chances of happiness but

Pause for *Thought*

The choice of 30 different collars is not a real choice in Marxist terms; it is just 30 slightly differentiated ways of becoming attached to *commodity fetishism* — the desire of the proletariat to buy or do fashionable things manufactured by the bourgeoisie as a means of exploiting the stupid, ignorant or poor. Think of London Fashion Week and *The X Factor*. How else does Fowles present ideas about exploitation in the novel?

it would appear that Fowles is suggesting that he can only grow as an individual when he does not belong to any particular interest group.

Peasantry and farmers

Peasantry and farmers are the most difficult group to categorise in the modern world. Marx thought of this group as essentially disorganised and largely incapable of effecting socio-economic change, believing that most would be forced into the proletariat as a consequence of social change such as land enclosures, while a few would become landlords. Mary begins life as a peasant but her marriage to the upwardly socially mobile Sam means that she becomes a member of the proletariat. Sarah too begins her life as 'a carter's daughter' but is educated out of her class.

Marxism and evolution

Marx saw human development in terms of evolutionary stages, though we need to remember Marx wrote *The Communist Manifesto* before Darwin published *The Origin of Species*, but *Capital* comes after both. The stages are as follows:

Taking it Further

Marxism still exerts a powerful influence on artists and intellectuals. On www.youtube.com listen to Billy Bragg's impromptu version of *The Internationale* (search for Billy Bragg Internationale) and to *Solidarity* by Angelic Upstarts (search for Angelic Upstarts Solidarity).

Both songs (lyrics available on www.lyricsfreak.com) are deeply concerned with ideas concerning freedom and empowerment, which is to be achieved via communal rather than individual action. How is it possible to describe both songs as bordering on the religious?

1 Primitive communism: as in pre-industrial tribal societies. Cooperation abounds.

2 Slave society: a development of tribal progression to city-state; aristocracy is foisted on the world.

3 Feudalism: aristocrats are the ruling class; merchants evolve into capitalists.

4 Capitalism: capitalists rule. They create and employ the proletariat.

5 Socialism: workers develop class consciousness and via proletarian revolution depose the capitalist dictatorship of the bourgeoisie, replacing it with a dictatorship of the working class, through which the socialisation of the means of production can be realised.

6 Communism: a classless and stateless society evolved from socialism. Happiness abounds.

Where Marx and Darwin differ significantly is that Marx believed that political development would naturally result in the creation of a communist society and that communism would represent the pinnacle of human happiness. Darwin placed no limits on evolution and certainly did not believe that any link in the evolutionary chain was either better or worse than any other link. Nature is indifferent. It is clear that, though Fowles finds much in Marx to admire, upsetting his neighbours in Lyme by threatening to vote Communist given the chance, he does not believe in 'the great full-stop' to human evolution.

Under capitalism the worker's entry into employment is voluntary in that the worker *chooses* which branch of capitalism to work for. However, essentially the worker must work or starve. Put another way, an individual must conform or perish, and capitalism, even with all of its shiny gewgaws, is another form of slavery: wage-slavery. Thus, exploitation is inevitable, and the voluntarism of capitalist exploitation is illusory. People who think capitalism is good for them (i.e. working-class people who vote Conservative) have what Marx termed 'false class-consciousness'. Capitalism makes people unhappy not just because of exploitation but because of *alienation*, by which Marx meant 'the estrangement of people from their humanity', a systematic result of capitalism. In Marxist analysis, alienation objectively describes the worker's situation within capitalism — self-awareness of this condition is unnecessary. Sarah at the beginning and Charles at the end of the novel are obviously alienated, as they are spiritually as well as physically displaced from their own humanity and are denied personal fulfilment.

The 'duty' of Marxists is to awaken in all members of the proletariat (and lumpenproletariat where possible) a sense of class-consciousness so that they can remove the dictatorship of capitalism in order to bring about socialism (and eventually communism) as quickly as possible. Marxism places a lot of emphasis on concepts such as duty and the conversion of those with 'false consciousness' and therefore has similarities to ideologies like Christianity. When Marx claimed 'Religion is the opium of the people' he was apparently unaware of any irony in the statement, not acknowledging or not aware of the religious nature of his new philosophy. Fowles finds much to admire in Marxist theory but he does not present Marxism as a philosophy which will make us truly free. For that the novelist recommends Existentialism.

Existentialism

Existentialism can perhaps be best explained as a world-view that opposes all philosophies which are based on the notion that in the arrangement of human affairs an ideal state can ever be reached. Existentialism claims that the individual is not an entity in, or the product of, any universal system but 'makes herself' as she goes along. The individual is not absolutely bound by nature, or heredity, or the concept of the immortal soul or concepts such as duty, because none of these concepts will determine what that individual really is. What a person really is can only be determined by 'existence' — the decisions the person takes and the consciously willed acts performed in the course of living. Most human beings perform no such acts and make no such

choices: being complicit in conformity, they are essentially nonentities, drifting and aimlessly following the decisions others make for them. In these ways they are like the lumpenproletariat identified by Marx.

The term 'Existentialism' was explicitly adopted as a self-description by French intellectual Jean-Paul Sartre (1905–1980) mentioned in Chapter 41 of the novel (p. 323). After World War II, the essential ingredients of Existentialism were widely disseminated through the literary and philosophical output of Sartre and his associates — notably his lover Simone de Beauvoir, Maurice Merleau-Ponty and Albert Camus. By the 1950s in many ways it had become a stance, a radical attitude towards life and society as much as a philosophy.

Sartre's Existentialism drew its immediate inspiration from German philosopher Martin Heidegger's *Being and Time* (1927), an inquiry into the 'being that we ourselves are' (which he termed *Dasein*: existence), which introduced most of the ideas that would characterise Existentialist thinking: the conflict between the private individual and the public citizen, a fascination with experiences of anxiety, the contemplation of death, the ideas of 'nothing' and nihilism, the rejection of religion and the advocacy of atheism, the distrust of science and its causal explanations as an adequate framework for understanding human beings, and the introduction of the idea of 'authenticity' as the norm of self-identity, tied to the idea of self-definition through freedom, choice, and commitment. Existentialism does not deny the validity of the basic categories of science. We obviously live in a world of matter, causality, force, function, organism, gravity, and so on. Existentialism claims that human beings cannot be *fully understood* in terms of science. Nor will moral theories suffice: intention, blame, responsibility, character, duty, virtue and the like do capture important aspects of the human condition but they do not fully explain to us the experience of existence.

Existentialism was as much a literary phenomenon as a philosophical one. Sartre's own ideas are even today better known through his fictional works such as *Nausea* (1938) and *No Exit* (*Huis Clos* in French, 1944) than through his more purely philosophical texts such as *Being and Nothingness* (1943) and *Critique of Dialectical Reason* (1960).

The heroes and heroines of Existentialist fiction, like Sarah Woodruff, realise at one point or another the necessity and importance of exercising their own free will.

Because Existentialist heroes nearly always fail in the attempt to give their lives authenticity via free will, Existentialism has frequently been labelled as a melancholy philosophy. However, Sarah does not fail in her quest to live a more authentic life than the one mapped out for her by

---

Pause for *Thought* ▮▮

On **www.youtube. com** listen to the Rush song 'Freewill*'* and read the lyrics at **www. lyricsfreak.com** via R — RU — Rush Lyrics — Freewill.

Compare and contrast the lyrics of 'Freewill' with the Matthew Arnold poem 'To Marguerite' found on p. 430 of the novel and the epigraph to Chapter 61 from Martin Gardner's *The Ambidextrous Universe* (p. 464). What do the three texts have to tell us about self-determination and self-responsibility? How are these ideas important in the context of the wider debate about freedom in *The French Lieutenant's Woman*?

her father, her education, her social class, and the Poulteneyish values of the stifling society into which she was born. Her efforts to self-actualise are successful — whether broadly or specifically will depend on the reader's analysis. Fowles claimed that his heroine had always behaved 'authentically' — a key term he borrows from Existentialism. Sarah, from the very outset of the novel, knows it is better to make an effort to take control of her own life than to acquiesce quietly to the control of others.

Authenticity leads to a set of questions: Do I succeed in making myself, or am I merely a function of the roles I find myself in? Am I *invented* by others? Thus, to be authentic can also be thought as a way of being autonomous. The inauthentic person, in contrast, merely *occupies* a role, and may do so 'irresolutely', without commitment. What is inherent in Existentialism is a rebellious streak and one of its defining features is protest: protest against academic philosophy, against establishment rules, against the 'iron in the soul' that is reason, against governments. Once we realise we are nothing, we can make the effort to become something. Many Existentialists committed themselves to left-wing causes because leftism is (or was seen to be in the 1940s and 1950s) anti-establishment and freedom-making. Leftism as an intellectual principle is still important in Existentialism, but hard-line Marxism was understood to be as deterministic and conformist as other religions and was eventually rejected because it preached that individuals were conditioned by socio-economic forces and so was as philosophically useless as Calvinism. Only free will, so the Existentialists claimed, can destroy the chains that bind us. Sarah Woodruff is clearly an example of a self-determining Existentialist rebel and by the time she lives in Rossetti's house has found a useful and fulfilling life. When Charles leaves her in Chapter 61 he has found faith in himself and has discovered a fuller Existentialist freedom than the one he had even when in America. In this context, Fowles's vision of Existentialism is not gloomy.

Sarah Woodruff is…an example of a self-determining Existentialist rebel

Working with the text

Meeting the Assessment Objectives

The four key English literature Assessment Objectives (AOs) describe the different skills you need to show in order to get a good grade. Regardless of what texts or what examination specification you are following, the AOs lie at the heart of your study of English literature at AS and A2; they let you know exactly what the examiners are looking for and provide a helpful framework for your literary studies.

The Assessment Objectives require you to:

- articulate creative, informed and relevant responses to literary texts, using appropriate terminology and concepts, and coherent, accurate written expression **(AO1)**
- demonstrate detailed critical understanding in analysing the ways in which structure, form and language shape meanings in literary texts **(AO2)**
- explore connections and comparisons between different literary texts, informed by interpretations of other readers **(AO3)**
- demonstrate understanding of the significance and influence of the contexts in which literary texts are written and understood **(AO4)**

Try to bear in mind that the AOs are there to support rather than restrict you; don't look at them as encouraging a tick-box approach or a mechanistic reductive way into the study of literature. Examination questions are written with the AOs in mind, so if you answer them clearly and carefully you should automatically hit the right targets. If you are devising your own questions for coursework, seek the help of your teacher to ensure that your essay title is carefully worded to liberate the required Assessment Objectives so that you can do your best.

Although the Assessment Objectives are common to all the exam boards, the specifications vary enormously in the way they meet the requirements. The boards' websites provide useful information, including sections for students, past papers, sample papers and mark schemes.

AQA: **www.aqa.org.uk**
EDEXCEL: **www.edexcel.com**
OCR: **www.ocr.org.uk**
WJEC: **www.wjec.co.uk**

Remember, though, that your knowledge and understanding of the text still lie at the heart of A-level study, as they always have done. While what constitutes a text may vary according to the specification you are following (e.g. it could be an article, extract, letter, diary, critical essay, review, novel, play or poem), and there may be an emphasis on the different ways texts can be interpreted and considering the texts in relation to different contexts, in the end the study of literature starts with, and comes back to, your engagement with the text itself.

Working with AO1

AO1 focuses upon literary and critical insight, organisation of material and clarity of written communication. Examiners are looking for accurate spelling and grammar and clarity of thought and expression, so say what you want to say, and say it as clearly as you can. Aim for cohesion; your ideas should be presented coherently with an overall sense of a developing argument.

Think carefully about your introduction, because your opening paragraph not only sets the agenda for your response but provides the reader with a strong first impression of you — positive or negative. Try to use 'appropriate terminology' but don't hide behind fancy critical terms or complicated language you don't fully understand; 'feature-spotting' and merely listing literary terms is a classic banana skin all examiners are familiar with. Choose your references carefully; copying out great gobbets of a text learned by heart underlines your inability to select the choicest short quotation with which to clinch your argument. Regurgitating chunks of material printed on the examination paper without detailed critical analysis is — for obvious reasons — a reductive exercise; instead try to incorporate brief quotations into your own sentences, weaving them in seamlessly to illustrate your points and develop your argument. The hallmarks of a well-written essay — whether for coursework or in an exam — include a clear and coherent introduction that orientates the reader, a systematic and logical argument, aptly chosen and neatly embedded quotations and a conclusion which consolidates your case

Working with AO2

In studying a text you should think about its overall form (novel, sonnet, tragedy, farce etc.), structure (how it is organised, how its constituent parts connect with each other) and language. In studying a long novel or a play it might be better to begin with the larger elements of form and structure before considering language, whereas analysing aspects of a poem's language (imagery, for example) might be a more appropriate place to start. If 'form is meaning', what are the implications of your chosen writer's decision to select this specific genre? In terms of structure, why does the on-stage action of one play unfold in real time while another spans months or years? In terms of language features, what is most striking about the diction of your text — dialogue, dialect, imagery or symbolism?

In order to discuss language in detail you will need to quote from the text — but the mere act of quoting is not enough to meet AO2. What is important is what you do with the quotation — how you analyse it and how it illuminates your argument. Moreover, since you will often need to make points about larger generic and organisational features of your chosen text such as books, chapters, verses, cantos, acts or scenes which are usually much too long to quote, being able to reference effectively is just as important as mastering the art of the embedded quotation.

Working with AO3

AO3 is a double Assessment Objective which asks you to 'explore connections and comparisons' between texts as well as showing your understanding of the views and interpretations of others. You will find it easier to make comparisons and connections between texts (of any kind) if you try to balance them as you write; remember also that connections and comparisons are not only about finding similarities — differences are just as interesting. Above all, consider how the comparison illuminates each text. It's not just a matter of finding the relationships and connections but of analysing what they show. When writing comparatively, use words and constructions that will help you to link your texts, such as 'whereas', 'on the other hand', 'while', 'in contrast', 'by comparison', 'as in', 'differently', 'similarly', 'comparably'.

To access the second half of AO3 effectively you need to measure your own interpretation of a text against those of your teacher and other students. By all means refer to named critics and quote from them if it seems appropriate, but the examiners are most interested in your personal and creative response. If your teacher takes a particular critical line, be prepared to challenge and question it; there is nothing more dispiriting for an examiner than to read a set of scripts from one centre which all say exactly the same thing. Top candidates produce fresh personal responses rather than merely regurgitating the ideas of others, however famous or insightful their interpretations may be.

Your interpretation will only be convincing if it is supported by clear reference to the text, and you will only be able to evaluate other readers' ideas if you test them against the evidence of the text itself. Worthwhile AO3 means more than quoting someone else's point of view and saying you agree, although it can be very helpful to use critical views if they push forward an argument of your own and you can offer relevant textual support. Look for other ways of reading texts — from a Marxist, feminist, new historicist, post-structuralist, psychoanalytic, dominant or oppositional point of view — which are more creative and original than merely copying out the ideas of just one person. Try to show an awareness of multiple readings with regard to your chosen text and an understanding that the meaning of a text is dependent as much upon what the reader brings to it as what the writer left there. Using modal verb phrases such as 'may be seen as', 'might be interpreted as' or 'could be represented as' implies that you are aware that different readers interpret texts in different ways at different times. The key word here is plurality; there is no single meaning, no right answer, and you need to evaluate a range of other ways of making textual meanings as you work towards your own.

Working with AO4

AO4, with its emphasis on the 'significance and influence' of the 'contexts in which literary texts are written and received', might at first seem less deeply rooted in the text itself but in fact you are considering and evaluating here the relationship between the text and its contexts. Note the word 'received': this refers to the way interpretation can be influenced by the specific contexts within which the reader is operating; when you are studying a text written many years ago, there is often an immense gulf between its original contemporary context of production and the twenty-first century context in which you receive it.

To access AO4 successfully you need to think about how contexts of production, reception, literature, culture, biography, geography, society, history, genre and intertextuality can affect texts. Place the text at the heart of the web of contextual factors that you feel have had the most

impact upon it; examiners want to see a sense of contextual alertness woven seamlessly into the fabric of your essay rather than a clumsy bolted-on rehash of a website or your old history notes. Try to convey your awareness of the fact that literary works contain embedded and encoded representations of the cultural, moral, religious, racial and political values of the society from which they emerged, and that over time attitudes and ideas change until the views they reflect are no longer widely shared. And you're right to think that there must be an overlap between a focus on interpretations (AO3) and a focus on contexts, so don't worry about pigeonholing the AOs here.

The four most important contextual frameworks in the novel have been Freudianism, Evolution, Marxism and Existentialism so these are useful tools for the student of *The French Lieutenant's Woman*. It is often helpful to see language as the map of a character's mind. Therefore A-level candidates who explore the language used by the characters (the direct speech a writer allocates them) as well as the writer's descriptive language outside of the speech marks enjoy far more success in exams than candidates who relay narrative without utilising text or who merely decorate the narrative with text. The following essay represents how a student may progress towards being able to write about the whole text by analysing smaller sections of the text. This sort of task is very useful practice for the kind of skills candidates are asked to demonstrate in practical criticism exams. The Assessment Objectives being examined via this task are AO1, AO2 and AO4.

Examination essay questions

More student essay answers are given as downloads on the free website at **www.philipallan.co.uk/literatureguidesonline**, including a comparative essay (for AO3).

Question 1

Sample question

> **Analyse Fowles's presentation of Charles and Sarah in Chapter 47 through a close exploration of their language on the first two pages.**

Student answer

A close analysis of Charles's and Sarah's language in Chapter 47 reveals to the reader many clues about their psychological state at this point in the novel. Charles's first words in the chapter after 'the radio-activity of guilt had crept through his nerves and veins' is to compare himself with both another man and his own high standards of behaviour: 'I am worse than Varguennes.' In Freudian terms his super-ego is evidently appalled at the behaviour of the id. Sarah on the other hand appears to exhibit no such moral qualms as she attempts to 'deny and hush him' with 'I cannot think beyond this hour.' She evidently feels that in a sense Time is standing still and her evident satisfaction at what has just happened is demonstrated through her acknowledgement that sex with Charles was a willed act — 'I wished it so.' Fowles reinforces her satisfaction at the sexual contact with the use of reiteration: 'I wished it so.' Her behaviour is of being Existentially happy within the moment, neither looking forward nor back: she first 'embraces' his hand and then 'presses it' to calm his rising guilt and so once again the novelist gives the impression that she is in control both of herself and of the situation.

In contrast to Sarah's low 'murmur' Charles's language is increasingly peppered with imperatives of duty, which illustrate his increasing anxiety: 'I must' is repeated twice when he considers his decision to break off his engagement with Ernestina. Sarah calmly tells him that she has 'been wicked. I have long imagined such a day as this', but when she tells him she is 'not fit' to be his wife the reader can detect Charles's confusion. She has seduced Charles yet he does not realise this and when she uses the term 'wicked' from the semantic field of morality the reader may begin to concede that even the enigmatic Sarah measures her life against conventional Victorian moral yardsticks. However, this is not the only analysis: an alternative interpretation is that she uses the term to communicate with the still-conventional Charles in the language he will understand and that her reference to her own wickedness is to provide him with a balm for his conscience, not to create a spike for her own. It is entirely possible that she may believe that she has not been wicked. She has lied to Charles continuously up to this point in the novel and the careful reader may assume she is still doing so now. Her reference to her imagination is significant if the reader analyses it in either its Freudian or Existentialist contexts: her imagination represents her hitherto repressed sexual desire for Charles, now achieved, the alignment of her id with her ego, or can be seen as an Existentialist outcome of free will and action. Her comment that she is 'not fit' to be his wife can be viewed in terms of the ongoing discourse within the novel concerning evolution: she is essentially a different species to Charles and cannot or will not fit herself into a convenient new form for him. She will not adapt to fit Charles's environment.

When Charles reverts to one of his stock phrases usually employed when he wants to patronise Ernestina 'My dearest —', the reader can see that in Marxist terms he is still assuming the bourgeois position of superior male to inferior female. Fowles's use of the dash makes it clear that Sarah interrupts him to tell him that marriage was impossible due to his 'position in the world', which reinforces the importance of Marxist class-consciousness, but, again, whether Sarah truly believes this is debatable. She may just want to get rid of him now that she has had her way with him and appeals to his self-interest. His references to his 'engagement', to 'blame' and to 'obligations' still show him to be a conventional Victorian man struggling in a moral vortex of trying to reconcile Desire with Duty. His cloying sentimentality is indiscriminate, as shown by the language he chooses to try to communicate affection: 'Sarah…it is the sweetest name.' He met a prostitute called Sarah only a few days ago in Chapter 39 and he did not find the name 'sweet' when he was vomiting into her pillow in Chapter 40. Charles lacks an adequate vocabulary for sexual love with a social equal and it is possible that Sarah finds all of these features of Charles's behaviour unappealing now that she has fulfilled her own sexual longing. Charles lacks the philosophical apparatus to comprehend that a woman may find a man sexually attractive but unappealing on an emotional level

Top ten **quotation** ❭

and the reader is reminded of the authorial observation made in Chapter 9 that Sarah 'was born with a computer in her heart' and that even here in bed with Charles her eyes are on 'some dark future'. The adjective is ominous for Charles. When Sarah continues to insist that she is not fit to marry Charles he grows increasingly baffled asking 'You cannot mean I should go away — as if nothing has happened between us?' but Sarah replies 'Why not, if I love you?' The careful reader will note that Sarah's 'declaration' of love is couched in a conditional phrase and, yet again, may not be true.

We are therefore left to conclude that Sarah has achieved what she has wanted since almost the first time that she saw Charles and has fulfilled a deep sexual longing and furthermore unlike Charles, still a 'fossil', she has evolved into a new species of Victorian woman: an active Existentialist schemer who has taken control of her own sexual life and successfully reconciled her id and her ego.

Examiner's comments

This is an outstanding essay. For AO1 the candidate demonstrates an excellent command of English. The terminology is always highly appropriate and used to support the candidate's exceptionally well-informed interpretations. The argument that Sarah is now existentially fulfilled due to her successful seduction of Charles but that he is still a 'fossil' is both sophisticated and compelling. References to Chapters

9, 39 and 40 show that the candidate has a sophisticated overview of the whole novel. Analysis of language (AO2) begins immediately and continues all the way through an essay which utilises 26 direct quotations in a succinct, integrated manner, never breaking up the candidate's smooth writing style. The essay is thoroughly convincing in demonstrating a perceptive understanding that language is the map of a character's mind; and the candidate displays a fine understanding of Fowles's techniques such as reiteration, Charles's use of imperative forms of verbs and his vapid reliance on patronising stock phrases to express what he imagines is genuine sentiment. The candidate is so aware of the nuances of language that she even analyses Fowles's use of the humble dash to indicate that Sarah is so in control of the situation and of herself that she feels confident and equal enough to interrupt a man. The candidate's abilities to contextualise the text are remarkable: Freud, Darwin and Marx are all here, as is a thorough knowledge of concepts such as Victorian notions of duty and obligation. Beyond all, the candidate shows mature understanding of the all-important context of Fowles's exploration of Existentialist freedom. This essay would be awarded full marks at A-level and is therefore the very highest grade A.

Question 2

Many examinations offer candidates the opportunity to offer transformational writing as a coursework task. Here is an example.

Sample question

> **Write Dr Grogan's journal entry following the events outlined in Chapter 53, giving his thoughts on Charles breaking his engagement to Ernestina. You should aim to create an authentic voice for Grogan which builds on Fowles's presentation of character and captures aspects of the novelist's form, structure and language.**

Student answer

By God didn't I give him a piece of my mind that young whippersnapper Smithson! Yet I cannot be too harsh on the fellow for he has given up a morsel in Mrs Tranters niece that many men would have devoured in monstrous fashion. So he is not quite the Mr Hyde that the young lady's father will make him out to be should this sordid matter come before the courts as I suppose it might. Rich men with Oxford Street shops do not like it when they feel they have been worsted in a business deal but like it even less when their little cherubs of daughters have been hurt by unscrupulous baronets with a taste for mad women who hang around the Cobb keeping

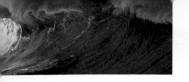

an eye out for caddish Frog navy types who've had their way and done a bunk back over the Channel. But that's woman for you: not entirely rational creatures when it comes to *amour*. I told Smithson the Woodruff woman was deranged and I even told him about Herr Doctor Hartmann's theories about hysterical girls with melancholia who made stories up to gain attention and as a cry for help. They do it with anorexia as well. Why, I thought the tale of Marie de Morrell would be enough to scare him out of his absurd fascination with la Woodruff. Woodruff was a governess just like that example of perfidious Albion Miss Allen. Poor women! Placed in occupations where they can see domestic bliss and yet not partake in it, not to have a share of it, not to live it. That is a hard punishment. And yet that is why they so often go a little mad. To put Matthei's text into his hand after grog and cigars, to have discussed the eminent Darwin and for Smithson to have spurned the advice burned into the pages in front of his eyes is outrageous! I thought he was one of the intellectual Elect but he was blinded by his desire for a woman who was fit for Exeter asylum more than to become the mistress of an ancient estate like Winsyatt.

I said I would horsewhip Smithson if he didn't get out of town within the hour. I did not mince matters because of the great harm he did to Miss Freeman. That pretty little moppet Mary was blubbering all over the place and I nearly had to give her a sedative so great was the noise that come out of her. Shrieking and balling like a banshee I thought she'd bring the roof in but Mrs Tranter calmed her down with a cuddle. There's three woman upset now because of Smithson so I didn't half give him what for with my barb about the Antinomian heresy: (Greek: anti against; nomos law) the group of early Christian heretics who argued that by faith and God's grace a Christian is freed from all laws (including the moral standards of the culture). Even the Worm of Wurms Martin Luther himself, despite his belief in *Sola Fide* (faith alone will be sufficient to secure Heaven) argued against antinomianism. I gave him my blood and thunder Dante rhetoric too but Smithson defended himself and I must conclude that he has been man enough to acknowledge that to have continued his engagement to Miss Freeman would have been for him to be imprisoned within a cruel lie — cruel for Smithson but doubly cruel for that gay linnet Miss Freeman — who would have no doubt renounced all happiness if she was forced to live with a man not completely devoted to her. There's strong metal in her small frame I'll be bound.

I pass here as a religious little fellow: the smiling Irishmen with a twinkle in his eye but I have never admired the Church of England and their little revolution that was no revolution. I could not have become a doctor without

to be seen playing the game in this seaside backwater and there is more than a mere memory of the old Faith about me — despite my scientific leanings. I believe myself to be a member of the rational and scientific elect and I know that Smithson wants to feel that he belongs to that exclusive Gentlemen's club too. The Elect as a term has links to Christianity. It occurs in the Gospels of Mark and Luke as well as several times in Matthew as a reference to believers in Christ who will be 'captured to Heaven' before the Great Tribulation of Judgement Day. I shouted at Smithson 'You won't be able to be thought of as a member of the elect unless you are able to introduce a finer and fairer morality into this dark world. If you do not you will be a mere despot.' Smithson looked sheepish once or twice as though being told off by his parents but when I told him he must become a 'better and more generous human being' to be 'forgiven' there was a look in his eye which showed he understood. If hunting Miss Freeman leads him into committing other sins I told him he would be 'more selfish…he is doubly damned'. I think he got what I was on about.

Now I shall take a drink of strong grog and espy the Nereids on the beach through the telescope should they deign to go perambulating at such an inclement time of year? That will settle my disordered thoughts. I shall puff on one of my Cuban cigars as I consider the folly of youth Tomorrow I shall keep a kindly eye on Miss Freeman and on poor Mrs Tranter, the saddest of all participants in this strange tale and I shall hope that young Smithson can find some joy if he manages ever to find the whereabouts of his mysterious French Lieutenant's Women.

Examiner's comments

The transformational voice here is often convincing. The references to Miss Freeman as a 'morsel' other men would have 'devoured in monstrous fashion', the awareness that Mr Freeman will consider a court case, sympathy with the plight of governesses, the well-placed references to Matthei and Hartmann, the contextualising of Darwin and definitions of the Elect, the references to 'grog', the telescope, the nereids and Dante are all persuasively Groganesque. Referring to Luther as the Worm of Wurms is amusing and could well fit Grogan's private thoughts about Protestantism. Similarly the candidate understands the doctor's sympathy for Mrs Tranter and Ernestina and shows a sensitive understanding of Charles's dilemma as a man who has broken a social code in order to maintain a personal and new-found morality.

Had there been no defects in this response all of the foregoing would have secured this essay a high reward. However, there are insecurities

and inconsistencies in the response. AO1 is occasionally wayward: the missing apostrophe in 'Tranter's' in line three is infelicitous as is the confusion over 'woman' and 'women' and 'Irishman' and 'Irishmen' at various points of the essay, the unVictorian contractions and modern phrases and terms such as 'done a bunk', 'cry for help', 'get out of town', 'shouted at', 'told off' and 'what I was on about' all jar. Occasionally grammatical errors such as missing punctuation undermine the sense of reliability the reader has in the response, and spelling errors can irritate: 'balled' for 'bawled'; 'hunting' for 'hurting' and 'Marie de *Morrell*' when the candidate should have written 'Marie de *Morell*' all betray an occasional carelessness which is not in keeping with the best A-level responses. The section on Mary would have been better placed in the preceding paragraph and the asides about Antinomianism and Christian interpretations of the Elect are merely bolted-on context (AO4), which would not occur in a *journal* of the Victorian or any other era: why would Grogan need to explain to himself concepts with which he was already extremely familiar? The candidate integrates the 'blood and thunder Dante rhetoric' far more convincingly, demonstrating she can contextualise effectively and seamlessly when she keeps her focus but the focus is not maintained: the examiner questions whether Grogan would use a term such as 'Frog navy types', as even Mrs Poulteney does not use such racist terms.

However, perhaps the most obvious defect with the work is its occasional howling anachronism. The reference to 'Cuban cigars' it could be argued is a little clumsy — Grogan keeps 'Burmah cheroots' in his 'cabin', but may well have Cuban cigars there too. Much more seriously, would Fowles have a character in 1867 refer to a book (*Strange Case of Doctor Jekyll and Mr Hyde*) not published until 1886? Fowles refers to Stevenson's novella in *The French Lieutenant's Woman* and presumably this confuses the candidate who evidently does not fully understand some of the techniques of Postmodern writing. The candidate also misuses her knowledge of Miss Allen. René Floriot in 1969 unearthed the truth about Miss Allen. Grogan has no way of knowing this in 1867. Though infelicities like these may look AO4 mistakes they are in fact more serious compound errors of AO4 *and* AO2. For this reason the candidate cannot be said to display much more than straightforward understanding of AO2. AO1 and AO4 are not sophisticated or systematic, due to their erratic profiles in the response, but are sometimes effective and sometimes relevant. On balance this AS response deserves a grade C.

Pause for *Thought*

Some candidates overuse technology and this candidate does so on two occasions. She gives the spelling of nereids as *Nereids* because the spell-checker has suggested it. Fowles uses the word with a lower case 'n' and the candidate would have been better advised to use Fowles's spelling. Also the correct biblical phrase describing the elevation of the elect into heaven is 'raptured', an unusual verb certainly; the spell-checker suggests 'captured' and the candidate agrees. So, trust the text not the technology!

Top ten quotations

Charles called himself a Darwinist, and yet he had not really understood Darwin. (Chapter 8, p. 50)

1

Fowles shows that knowledge which we can not apply to help us understand or improve the human condition is itself fossilised. This is an Existentialist critique of all science. Significantly Charles drops his interest in science and discovers a passion for literature after Sarah abandons him.

She was born with a computer in her heart. (Fowles about Sarah, Chapter 9, p. 53)

2

Sarah is presented as a woman with 1960s' values and sensibilities trying to understand the 1860s. She is thus ahead of her time in her abilities to compute, plan, arrange and order her own life. This is a very early clue to Sarah's calculating nature.

...I live among people the world tells me are kind, pious, Christian people. And they seem to me crueller than the cruellest heathens, stupider than the stupidest animals. (Sarah to Charles, Chapter 18, p. 142)

3

Sarah expresses her sense of frustrated alienation from English society. In this passionate appeal to Charles she tries to explain why she has *chosen* the role of outcast. In Existentialist terms, if society is a trap, Sarah has to move beyond it to become free.

Why am I born what I am? Why am I not born Miss Freeman? (Sarah to Charles, Chapter 18, p. 142)

4

When Sarah asks this question Charles thinks she is committing the Victorian sin of envying someone in a higher social class, but Sarah claims she asks the question due to incomprehension: why, when she has equal or superior talents to Ernestina, is life so much harder for Sarah? The question has as much to do with Marxism as Existentialism.

You cannot [understand]...Because you are not a woman who was born to be a farmer's wife but educated to be something... better....It came to seem to me as if I were allowed to live in paradise, but forbidden to enjoy it...I have a freedom [other women] cannot understand. No insult, no blame can touch me. (Sarah to Charles, Chapter 21, pp. 170 and 176)

5

Sarah here demonstrates her dual nature or a sense of *before* and *after*. She was excluded from the fruits of life by a class system that used her education as a tool to benefit others, not herself. Afterwards to avoid the pain her partial exclusion brings she removes herself altogether and by becoming a sexual outcast achieves a kind of freedom. In Existentialist terms life is for living. Merely to observe it is to be imprisoned.

6 **...excited...to the very roots of his being...He knew if he reached out his arms he would meet with no resistance... only a passionate reciprocity of feeling. The red in his cheeks deepened, and at last he whispered. 'We must never meet alone again.' (Fowles about Charles/Charles to Sarah, Chapter 21, pp. 186–87)**

Charles becomes aware that his desire for Sarah is reciprocated but will overwhelm him. He clings to the idea of 'duty' via the use of the moral imperative 'must', yet chooses to meet Sarah alone on two more occasions after this when he kisses her in Chapter 31 and in Chapter 46 when he has sex with her, each time in response to a note sent by Sarah.

7 **Destiny.**

Those eyes. (Fowles about Sarah, Chapter 28, p. 238)

Fowles shows via Freud and Darwin that sex is our adult destiny. Charles thinks he has choice but he may be an unthinking ammonite. At the halfway point of the novel the author is asking whether Charles's emerging Existentialist awareness that he must exercise free will can conquer his march towards extinction. Can he *naturally select* himself to survive?

8 **To postpone such desire for a week, a month, a year, several years even, that can be done. But for eternity is when the iron bites. (Fowles about Charles, Chapter 46, p. 350)**

Fowles communicates the impossibility of denying the id and acting against our own human nature.

9 **You have given me the consolation of believing that in another world, another age, another life, I might have been your wife. (Sarah to Charles, Chapter 47, p. 358)**

Sarah here confesses her motivation for seducing Charles. Unaware he has been seduced, Charles does not understand that Sarah willed the act so she can self-actualise and fulfil her sexual desires.

10 **...freed from his age, his ancestry and class and country, he [Charles] had not realised how much the freedom was**

embodied in Sarah...He no longer much believed in that
freedom; he felt he had merely changed traps, or prisons.
But...However bitter his destiny, it was nobler than that
one he had rejected. (Fowles about Charles, Chapter 58,
pp. 430–31)

Towards the end of the novel, Charles is now an outcast, as Sarah was at
the beginning, and realises the pain his rebellion has brought. However,
because his Existentialist awareness is now complete, he knows that his
rejection of Ernestina and Freemanism was the difficult but authentic
choice to have made. From now Charles has the 'atom of faith in himself'
he needs to 'endure' and hopefully, one day, enjoy life.

Taking it further

Fiction

The following novels are excellent companions to *The French
Lieutenant's Woman*:

- Fowles, John (1963) *The Collector*, Jonathan Cape.
- Fowles, John (1965) *The Magus* (revised 1977), Jonathan Cape.
- Hardy, Thomas (1891) *Tess of the d'Urbervilles*, Penguin Classics 2003.
- Hardy, Thomas (1895) *Jude the Obscure*, Penguin Classics 2009.
- Alain-Fournier (1913) *Le Grand Meaulnes*, Penguin Modern Classics
  2000.

Criticism

The following critical works are interesting:

- Bradbury, Malcolm (3 August 1980) *'The French Lieutenant's Woman'*,
  Observer Review.
- Conradi, Peter (1982) *John Fowles*, Methuen.
- Mansfield, Elizabeth (1981) 'A Sequence of Endings: the manuscripts of
  "The French Lieutenant's Woman" ', *Journal of Modern Literature 8:2*,
  John Fowles Special.

- Mason, Michael (27 November 1981) 'Good fiction and bad history, Review of "The French Lieutenant's Woman" ', *Times Literary Supplement*.
- Watt, Ian (9 November 1969) 'A Traditional Victorian Novel? Yes and Yet … Review of "The French Lieutenant's Woman" ', *New York Times Book Review*.
- Bennett, Tony (1979) *Formalism and Marxism*, Methuen.
- Bradbury, Malcolm (ed.) (1977) *The Novel Today: Contemporary Writers on Modern Fiction*, Fontana.
- Loveday, Simon (1985) *The Romances of John Fowles*, Macmillan.

Websites

- The John Fowles Website **www.fowlesbooks.com**
  — This is a site run and maintained by Fowles's devotees and is a splendid embarkation point for anyone interested in Fowles.
- Library Thing **www.librarything.com**
  — This is the world's largest book club, which can put you in touch with people who have 'eerily similar tastes' to your own. The discussion forum pages on Fowles are lively and opinionated.

DVDs

- *The French Lieutenant's Woman* (1981) directed by Karel Reisz, screenplay by Harold Pinter, is an excellent adaptation of the film. With strong performances from Meryl Streep and Jeremy Irons, Fowles called the film a 'beautiful metaphor' for his novel. The film won a raft of awards: hugely enjoyable.
- *The Collector* (1965) directed by William Wyler, screenplay by Stanley Mann and John Kohn, features excellent performances from Terence Stamp as Clegg and Samantha Eggar as Miranda, nominated for a best actress Oscar for her performance: very enjoyable.
- *The Magus* (1968) directed by Guy Green, screenplay by John Fowles, was described by Michael Caine, who played Nicholas Urfe, as 'One of the worst three movies I've ever been in (the other two were *Ashanti* and *The Swarm*). No-one had a clue what it was about.' However, it has slowly and unexpectedly become a cult classic, especially with students, thus prompting its release as a DVD in 2006. Watch out for Fowles himself as a sailor in the opening credits. The film is interesting, especially in the light of its controversial history.